Welsh language *cynghanedd* poetry, whether solemn or scurrilous, is one of the unsung glories of European civilization. A stunning edifice of aural architecture, it is an acoustic environment that has long reverberated to all the mood music of the human imagination. In this engaging and authoritative study Mererid Hopwood provides the key to a secret world of sound that may be found as readily in a modern Welsh pub as in the ancient halls of the Welsh princes. Beginners are admitted by seductive degrees to the magic circle of the chaired bards – the *cynghanedd* poets.

Professor M. Wynn Thomas
University of Wales Swansea

Singing in Chains

Listening to Welsh Verse

Mererid Hopwood

gomer

First Impression – 2004
Second Impression – 2005

ISBN 1 84323 402 5

© Mererid Hopwood

This book is published with the financial support
of the Welsh Books Council.

Printed in Wales at
Gomer Press, Llandysul, Ceredigion SA44 4JL

I Mam
am helpu Dad i ddod yn Gymro

ACKNOWLEDGEMENTS

Diolch i

Martin a'r plant am eu cefnogaeth
Dafydd a Wynn am eu cyngor
Ceri am ei amynedd a'i gymorth parod
Dylan am ei anogaeth

CONTENTS

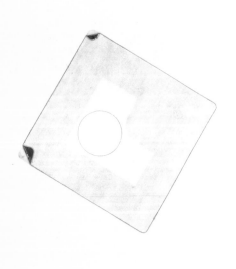

INTRODUCTION

There is a certain art form in Wales that doesn't exist in any other culture. It is a special kind of literary form that is classed as poetry, but it is also one that lies very close to music. It is known in Welsh as *cynghanedd* or *cerdd dafod* or *canu caeth*. The last of these terms – *canu caeth* – literally translated means the 'captive' or 'confined' song, and it is so called because of the set of complex rules that underpins it. This is the art form that is the very essence of the poetic tradition of Wales. And before one can express oneself in *cynghanedd*, one has to learn the theory and obey its code.

Dewi Emrys, poet and author of a seminal textbook on *cynghanedd* once wrote:

> *Cynghanedd* is a Science. By this it is meant that *cynghanedd* is not something which happens by accident or whim. It is completely constant and true to itself like the maxims of Euclid.
>
> A rhymester can manage to compose a verse or doggerel from his own head by natural talent or in imitation of a verse he might know. But no one has ever succeeded in writing *cynghanedd* in this free manner. The art must be learnt exactly in the same way as every craft that demands detailed apprenticeship.[1]

But *cynghanedd* is much more than a science and much, much more than a set of complex rules. As the last sentence of the quotation above reveals, it is both art and craft. And though it can be argued that, once upon a time, these two words meant the same, today 'art' is usually understood as having the added ingredient of being something brought about by some kind of 'muse' or 'creative spirit'. By bringing 'art' and 'craft' together in one breath, Dewi Emrys reveals the very deep appreciation that exists in Wales of the craft of poetry and the awareness that while there can be craft without art, there can never be art without craft. One can master the craft of *cynghanedd* and thus become a *prydydd* without however

[1] Translated from *Odl a Chynghanedd*, Dewi Emrys, London (1938), p. 111.

becoming a *bardd*. Both titles are translated by the English word
'poet', but in Welsh the term *bardd* distinguishes the artist from the
craftsman.[2]

Of course there is more to poetry than the technical considerations
of such things as rhyme, assonance and rhythm, but there is no
poetry without them – though not, necessarily, all of them at once!
Similarly, there is more to prose than grammar and there is more to
music than rhythm and pitch. These are the rudiments of the crafts
that underpin the art forms.

The craft behind works composed in *cynghanedd* or *canu caeth*
is spelt out in the rules of *cerdd dafod*. The code that embraces
these rules is a tool in the poet's hand, but it is such a nimble tool
and so essential that, in a master's hand, at times it can almost seem
as if the tool itself is creating the art.

As well as being highly crafted, *cynghanedd* is highly popular in
Wales. Enjoyed by young and old alike, it has a following like no
other literary form in the country. Poets who practise the art can
perform their work to packed halls. Indeed, poetry in general is in
no way elitist in Wales and it is encouraged from a very young age.
We have a children's 'poet laureate' (with pin-up posters to match)
and the annual poetry competitions at our cultural festivals – the
eisteddfodau – are widely covered in the media. *Cynghanedd* is
taught to a certain extent through the conventional educational
streams – schools and universities – but its main breeding ground is
in more informal night-classes, where people come together in
village halls, chapel vestries and pubs to learn its mysteries.

People who have themselves not acquired the craft of *cynghanedd*
often question its restrictive nature. They see the rules as a barrier
to creativity. They forget that art relies on the mastery of craft. One
cannot hope to create meaningful music out of a Chopin piano
concerto without having mastered scales and arpeggios. One
cannot hope to produce the Mona Lisa without mastery of line and
form. While learning the craft behind any art form can be hard work,
once mastered it is a discipline that liberates the creative spirit. It
does not hold this spirit back. On the contrary, it gives it wings.

---

[2] It must be noted however, that the usage of these terms has changed
over time. Once upon a time they meant precisely the opposite and
prydydd was by far the superior title.

Take language. If we had to stop and consider the complexities of the simplest passage of conversation – from the tense and mode of the verb to its conjugation; from the effect of preposition on pronouns to the choice of vocabulary – then I believe we might be too afraid to speak at all. Yet, we have all managed to grasp these complexities and so, potentially, are in a position to express virtually the whole range of our experiences. The same is true of *cynghanedd*. Once its 'grammar' has been learnt it is as fluid as language and as agile as song. It enables the creative mind to say precisely what it has to say in a most beautiful poetic form.

Over the next few chapters, I shall try to outline the development of this ancient, yet thoroughly modern tradition, before moving on to explain the most basic principles of how it works. The examples in the exercises can be read and heard in the accompanying CD. So too can the poems presented throughout the book.

But before we start, one thing needs to be stressed. This is not a book for the timid or for the half-hearted! There is no quick fix to learn *cynghanedd*. In this age of instant-gardens, two-hour transformations of houses and humans, and even 'Welsh in a Week', this is one area where time must play its part. There are no short cuts. In the days of the professional court poet in Wales, it was deemed that it would take any would-be poet approximately nine years to learn the craft. And to this day, those who manage to master *cynghanedd* in a shorter space of time are rare. It has certainly been my experience that the more you know about it, the more you realise you don't know. And after nine years, I'm still learning. To those who persist, I hope they will find it enlightening and fun!

CHAPTER 1

Accident and Design

When the nineteenth-century Spanish poet, José de Espronceda, composed the line: *y tus besos hielo son* ('and your kisses are made of ice'), I cannot imagine that he was aware that this line obeyed exactly the highly complex rules of the ancient tradition of Welsh verse. Instead, I suspect, it was his poetic instinct that told him that this was a beautiful line. It was musically pleasing to his ear. And so it is! Try saying it out aloud, slowly: *y tus besos hielo son.* Phonetically – i tʊs besɒs ielɒ sɒn.

I imagine that it was the same story when Goethe, back in the late 1700s, described the river in his poem *An Den Mond* ('Ode to the Moon') musing thus: *Fließe, fließe, lieber Fluß!,* or phonetically, flisʌ flisʌ l\u0256ɛr flʊs, which means 'Flow, flow on, lovely river!'. His well-trained ear assured the instincts of this great German poet that here was an irresistibly musical line.

When Millevoye, again in the late eighteenth century, wrote about death saying: *Le silence du mausolée,* or phonetically, lʌ silɒns dʊ məʊsɒleɪ, which means 'The silence of the mausoleum', it is highly improbable that he had ever heard of the Welsh tradition. It is much more likely that it was his natural flair and his experience as a poet that made him choose this particular sequence of words as opposed to all other possible arrangements. And the same can surely be said of Chaucer in the fourteenth century as he composed the line 'And ship and man under the water wente'.

While each of these lines is written in a different language and at different times by different poets, they share a common signature. Unbeknown to their authors, they contain *cynghanedd*, a term that is translated into English by a rather ugly phrase: 'Welsh strict metre'. But *cynghanedd* is a word that, in its essence, quite simply means 'harmony'. And while *cynghanedd* is indeed the technical term for the complicated rules of our poetic tradition, recognising that it truly means 'harmony' might help to understand the timeless appeal of this form of composition.

1

In the first instance, *cynghanedd*, understood as 'harmony', takes us to the field of music. If we accept that poetry happens somewhere on the border between the fields of prose and music, and somewhere between speech and song, then we can accept that lines of poetry may be harmonized. In the Welsh literary tradition the very best poet was always known as the *Pencerdd*. While in the old days this term might be best translated as the 'Master Craftsman', today a literal translation would be the 'Chief-of-Song'. The switch in meaning is significant, for in it we can begin to realise how much importance is placed in Wales on the 'music' of a line of poetry. To this day, to tell a Welsh poet that his or her line 'sings' is high praise indeed. And to this day too, a poem is known in Welsh as *cerdd*, where *cerddoriaeth*, in English, is 'music'. And, as already mentioned in the 'Introduction', the code, in which the rules for this musical and magical form of composition are laid down, is known as *cerdd dafod* (literally: 'the music, or craft, of the tongue').[1]

Secondly, the word *cynghanedd* understood as 'harmony', suggests that a line of poetry, like a line of harmonized music, can move in two directions, and perhaps this is the key to understanding what makes a line written in *cynghanedd* so special.

Many literary traditions the world over recognise that a line of poetry moves along from A to B, following the ordinary horizontal direction of speech. Take Robert Frost's 'The Road Not Taken':

> Two roads diverged in a yellow wood
> And sorry I could not travel both
> And be one traveler, long I stood
> And looked down one as far as I could
> To where it bent in the undergrowth.

---

[1] This, in turn, co-exists with another complex code – this time, a code of music as other cultures might recognise music, in that it relates primarily to the singing of poems to the accompaniment of the harp – which is known as *cerdd dant* (literally: 'the music, or craft, of the string'). The principles of *cerdd dant* are based on the stress structures of the poem it sets to music. See chapter 3 for further treatment of this notion of 'stress'.

Here the words at the end of the line act as magnets and draw the reader towards them. The rhyme between the last words of each line (in this instance, in a pattern a b a a b) gives the magnet added strength.

This can be compared to an unharmonized piece of music – where the single line of the melody draws the listener towards the end of the phrase:

But let us add harmony to this melody:[2]

This time, the listener hears in two directions: horizontally, towards the end of the phrase, and vertically, through the chords.

This is what happens when you compose a line of *cynghanedd* – the sound of the line is multi-layered; it is almost as if it moves in two directions. The meaning of the line, and the end-rhyme, for there is almost always an end-rhyme, draws the listener from its beginning to its end. (Note that your target audience is imagined primarily as a 'listener' not a 'reader'.) But the internal harmony between the words as they co-exist in varied, but highly organised, patterns of rhyme, assonance, alliteration and consonance, demands that the listener hears in other directions too.

As the examples at the beginning of this chapter show, lines of *cynghanedd* can be found in literary traditions all over the world, but, as suggested, where they occur in the work of poets outside Wales, it can be assumed that they have been composed without an

[2] 'Cwm Rhondda', John Hughes.

awareness of any rules. Of course, this is not to say that their
creation is entirely by accident. They come about as the result of
the poet's instinct and their validity is endorsed by the poet's
experience. In Wales, however, the composition of such lines is
deliberate. Over the centuries, it is as if a particular code of musical
poetry has been cracked and the reasons for the music in such lines
have been articulated. In turn, they have been transformed into
rules, rules that have grown out of the experience of generations of
poets who have learnt the secrets of what makes a line of spoken
words 'sing'.

Much has been written in English about the complexity of
cynghanedd, and time and again it is said that the Welsh language
lends itself to *cynghanedd* in a way that English (in particular) does
not. It is said that the stress patterns of Welsh and the way the
language mutates words (i.e. changes the first letter of words
according to their gender, place and function in a sentence), makes
the potential for *cynghanedd* greater in Welsh than in English.

But these arguments miss the point. The Welsh language and
cynghanedd have developed hand in hand. Each is an integral part
of the other. Ultimately, anyone who genuinely wants to understand
this unique tradition will have to learn Welsh. By the same token,
anyone who wants to master the Welsh language and become truly
immersed in its nuances will have to address the importance of
cynghanedd and the poetic tradition to its development. The
rhythms of poetry have affected speech patterns and vice-versa. As
an English journalist concluded back in 1939:

> . . . this universal love and practice of poetry in Wales is inseparable
> from the language itself. Your language is, therefore, something
> more than words on your lips. It is the life-blood of your peculiar
> culture.[3]

Patterns can be illustrated in English, examples can be given and
rules can be learnt. But even those who wish to learn the craft of
composing *cynghanedd* **in Welsh** need more than a handbook.
They need a forum, an audience of experienced listeners, and
ideally a teacher at hand, in order to try out their lines and gauge
reactions. It is, after all, an oral and aural tradition.

[3] From the introduction to *Beirdd y Babell,* Dewi Emrys, Wrecsam (1939).

I use the term 'experienced listeners' because I feel that this makes an important point. It gives another reason why *cynghanedd* doesn't really work in other cultures, for the full appreciation of *cynghanedd* demands almost as much experience from the listener as it does from the poet. Just as English listeners (or readers) will appreciate the punch in a closing line of a limerick or the sense of resolution in the rhyming couplet at the end of a sonnet, Welsh-speaking listeners will appreciate *cynghanedd*. The majority might not be able to explain why such and such a line is so effective, or what accounts for the satisfying melody in such and such a couplet, but the appreciation of it will come from being immersed in the culture that has made *cynghanedd* possible. Their experience will have taught them anticipation which is there for the poet to indulge or challenge!

I imagine that hearing *cynghanedd* to a non-Welsh speaker must be akin to my experience when I hear a piece of Chinese music. I can sense its beauty but I don't really understand it. I can't hum the tune. Often I'm not really sure whether I should feel happy or sad.

So why bother to write a book about *cynghanedd* in English if it can only really be understood once you have learnt Welsh? The truthful answer might be naïve. I suppose my hope is that it may open the ears of those, ignorant of our culture, who have settled in our midst. I hope that it will begin to open their eyes and kindle in them a desire to learn Welsh.

And it is this thought process that has led me to abandon the notion of composing whole exercises in English. Rather, I have decided to use *cynghanedd* as a way into the Welsh language. After finishing reading this book, I hope that the reader will have at least learnt some Welsh – and more importantly, been encouraged to learn more – even if he or she has not grasped the rudiments of the craft!

CHAPTER 2

A Strategy for Immortality

Cynghanedd doesn't have a birthday. It wasn't born. It was distilled. And the first record we have which hints at *cynghanedd* is in work composed in a language we can recognise as Welsh, even though it belongs to an area that straddles southern Scotland and northern England. In those days, back in the sixth and seventh centuries, we know that four regions within this land were called respectively *Ystrad Clud* (the Vale of Clyde), *Rheged* (Wigtown and Kirkudbright), *Gododdin* (between the rivers Forth and Tyne), and *Elfed* (around the town of Leeds). This was a land of warriors, a land that the local Brythonic people had to defend against invaders from the North and the East. The deeds of many of these battles have been lost in the mists of time, but the work of two war correspondents, two poets, has ensured that the fates of some of the victors and vanquished are remembered to this day.

Taliesin and Aneirin were virtual contemporaries, although we do not know if the two ever met. Their poems depicting the harsh realities of the time are amongst the earliest extant examples of European literature, and their words still inspire today. These poets knew how to use rhyme and alliteration to great effect, and although *cynghanedd* would not be formalized for a few more centuries, the beginnings of this art form are already here in the lines of Aneirin and Taliesin. Thus we are reminded that the beginnings of Welsh, the beginnings of Welsh poetry and the beginnings of *cynghanedd* are inextricably linked.

When one of the Brython warriors fell in battle, Taliesin composed an elegy, *'Marwnad Owain ab Urien'*. Owain was a fighter feared by his enemies, but to his own people he was a revered hero. In the elegy, Taliesin depicts a scene where the enemy lay dead, having been slain by Owain's men:

> *Cysgid Lloegr llydan nifer*
> *A lleufer yn eu llygaid.*

> Sleepeth the wide host of England
> With light in their eyes.[1]

The repetition of the '*ll*' sound – *Lloegr*, *llydan*, *lleufer*, *llygaid* – together with the rhyme between the end of the first line and the middle of the second, *nifer* / *lleufer*, show early hints of *cynghanedd*. These sounds echo one another creating a layered music as Taliesin conveys the anguish of war relating as much to the tears of defeat as the joys of victory.

This alliteration and assonance is a strategy for immortality. After all, one of the reasons for the longevity of the Welsh literary tradition is that its components have been memorable. This is essential for the continuation of an oral tradition. The successful passing of poems and stories by word of mouth from one generation to the next established the collective memory of a people. It follows that epic stories – whether in poetry or prose – were constructed in such a way that they were relatively easy to remember. One of these strategies in prose was to relate elements of the stories in groups of three. The earliest record of such a grouping is '*Trioedd y Meirch*' from *Llyfr Du Caerfyrddin* ('The Black Book of Carmarthen'), which is a list of the names of the horses of ancient Welsh heroes. In poetry, the most important strategy was the use of *cynghanedd*. Its internal rhymes and alliteration helped to direct the memory from one word to the other, enabling young and old alike to remember events and people who would otherwise have been lost to oblivion.

In this example from '*Y Gododdin*', where Aneirin describes a bloody battle in *Catraeth* (Catterick), he uses alliteration to lead the listener from one line to the next:

> *Ein cedwyr am Gatraeth ry-wnaeth **brith**red,*
> ***Brith**we adwyar sathar sanged*

> Our warriors did battle around Catraeth,
> Blood-stained clothes were trodden down[2]

---

[1] *Welsh Verse*, Tony Conran, Bridgend (2003), p. 112.
[2] *Aneirin: Y Gododdin*, A. O. H. Jarman, Gomer (1988).

and in this next line (perhaps the most widely remembered of them all) the internal rhyme guides the memory from the verb to the place name to the adjective:

*Gwyr **aeth** Gatr**aeth** oedd ff**raeth** eu llu*

Men went to Catraeth, keen was their company[3]

Another example of an early version of *cynghanedd* is found in the Llywarch Hen cycle. Llywarch Hen is a Welsh hero and in a moving poem from the ninth century, Llywarch, by now an old man who had seen his twenty-four sons die in battle, is compared to a withered leaf:

Y ddeilen hon, neus cynired gwynt,
Gwae hi o'i thynged:
Hi hen, eleni ganed.

This leaf, driven here and there by the wind,
Woe to it for its fate.
It is old. This year it was born.[4]

Notice the last line of the stanza: '*Hi hen, eleni ganed.*' Here, as in the work of Taliesin and Aneirin, we hear the rhyme and internal matching of consonants that is *cynghanedd* as we know it today, though this line is well over a thousand years old. We find rhymes binding the words: *cynired / thynged / ganed* and *hen / eleni*, and we find the consonant '*n*' binding three words in the third line: *hen / eleni / ganed*.

So when did these patterns become regulated? When did this early poetic instinct become formalized, almost a scientific theory that would ensure that lines could be passed on from generation to generation? It is difficult to tell. No one can be sure who was the very first to record the measures of this ancient craft, but Dafydd Morgannwg notes that one of the earliest to do so was Asser Menevenses, a ninth-century scholar and teacher to Alfred the

[3] *Ibid* p. 114.
[4] Dafydd Johnston *The Literature of Wales – A Pocket Guide* Cardiff (1994), p. 12.

Great.[5] It is believed that he was a grandchild of the great king Rhodri Fawr and came from Pencaer in North Pembrokeshire, where the little hamlet of Trefasser bears his name to this day. According to Dafydd Morgannwg, Asser was also known as Geraint Fardd Glas. Be that as it may, it is certain that as early as the tenth century, Hywel Dda,[6] the enlightened king and law-maker, had defined the privileged status of poets and codified a bardic order in Wales.

It is also certain that by the twelfth century there was enough standardization of verse craft to make it possible to hold competitions to find out who was the most skilled and well-trained poet. This is a custom upheld to the present day in the local and national cultural festivals known as the eisteddfodau.

But before we consider that first national (or indeed international) eisteddfod held in Cardigan in 1176, let us look at the role of the poet in this period, for it should be realized that from the very beginning, the poet has enjoyed special status in Wales. Taliesin himself became the subject matter of a legend – *Hanes Taliesin* – that links him to the birth of the Muse. This story tells of how young Gwion, the servant boy, accidentally swallowed three drops from the magic potion made in the cauldron of Ceridwen the witch. This transformed him into various animals until finally he was reincarnated as Taliesin, the very first poet. Taliesin literally means 'beautiful forehead' and this attribute is a mark of the powers of prophecy that were often expected of poets!

Poets practising in the twelfth century are known as *Beirdd y Tywysogion* – the poets of the princes. (It is customary to consider the Welsh poetic tradition according to the work of different 'ages' of poets. The earliest are known as the *Cynfeirdd*, the early poets; then come the *Gogynfeirdd*, the fairly early poets; followed by the next 'age', the poets of the princes.) These were the medieval poets and they were closely associated with the three royal kingdoms of Wales: Gwynedd in the north, Powys in mid-Wales and Deheubarth in the south.

---

[5] See Dafydd Morgannwg's seminal handbook on *cynghanedd* – *Yr Ysgol Farddol* ('The Bardic School').

[6] Some of the laws of Hywel Dda were in force in Wales until after the Conquest by Edward I and are considered to be amongst the most enlightened in Europe of their time.

The bardic profession was structured like no other.[7] First and most important came the *Pencerdd* (literally, as already noted, 'chief-of-song'), then came the *Bardd Teulu* (literally 'poet to the household') and lowest in rank was the *Cerddor* (literally 'the musician').

The *Pencerdd* was expected to declaim poems to God and to the king, and was honoured for his services with a special chair in the royal court. The *Bardd Teulu* was an officer in court (one of twenty-four) and as such was expected to perform his work before battle and entertain the queen. It is not entirely clear what the role of the *Cerddor* was, but it is certain that poets in each of the categories had both a formal and an informal function and that theirs was not merely the role of entertainer, but also that of chronicler and oral archivist. They were trained professionals with a relatively formal pay structure[8] and their nine-year training familiarised the apprentices with the Welsh poetic tradition, and its practice enabled them to recall ancient compositions.

With a bardic order in place, it is no wonder that it occurred to Rhys ap Gruffudd, Lord Rhys of Dinefwr, to initiate a competition to find out who had mastered the rules, who could show the most skill and who indeed was the best poet. In 1176, poets were invited from all parts of Wales, England, Scotland and Ireland to take part in this first eisteddfod, held in Cardigan. And a record in the ancient book *Brut y Tywysogion* notes that it was the contingent from Gwynedd that showed the most dexterity in the craft of *cerdd dafod*.

Just over a century later, 1282 was a fateful year. Llywelyn ap Gruffudd (known in Wales as 'Llywelyn ein Llyw Olaf',[9] a title that is itself a line of *cynghanedd*) is killed by the English, and his death in effect, marks the end of the political independence of Wales. This tragedy inspires Gruffydd ab yr Ynad Coch to write an

[7] While there was no comparable system in England there is some parallel with the Irish bardic order of the time, though this was even more of a closed shop.

[8] A tract dating from the early sixteenth century known as *Statud Gruffudd ap Cynan* notes to the penny the rates of pay for various verse measures, but it was also common to offer poets useful tools such as an axe or sword as payment.

[9] *Llywelyn ein Llyw Olaf* – 'Llywelyn our Last Leader'.

elegy that to this day is considered one of the finest in the Welsh
language:

> *Poni welwch-chwi hynt y gwynt a'r glaw?*
> *Poni welwch-chwi'r deri'n ymdaraw?*
> *Poni welwch-chwi'r môr yn merwinaw'r tir ?*
> *Poni welwch-chwi'r gwir yn ymgyweiriaw?*
> *Poni welwch-chwi'r haul yn hwyliaw'r awyr?*
> *Poni welwch-chwi'r sêr wedi syrthiaw?*
> *Poni chredwch-chwi i Dduw, ddyniadon ynfyd?*
> *Poni welwch-chwi'r byd wedi'r bydiaw?*
> *Och hyd atat-Ti, Dduw, na ddaw môr tros dir!*
> *Pa beth y'n gedir i ohiriaw?*
> *Nid oes le y cyrcher rhag carchar braw,*
> *Nid oes le y triger: och o'r trigaw!*

> See you not the way of the wind and the rain?
> See you not the oak trees buffet together?
> See you not the sea stinging the land?
> See you not truth in travail?
> See you not the sun hurtling through the sky,
> And that the stars are fallen?
> Do you not believe God, demented mortals?
> Do you not see the whole world's danger?
> Why, O my God, does the sea not cover the land?
> Why are we left to linger?
> There is no refuge from imprisoning fear,
> And nowhere to bide – O such abiding! . . .[10]

In this poem we see how the patterns of rhyme and alliteration have
become more complex and how they weave their way through the
poem. Let's examine the first four lines:

*Poni welwch-chwi h<u>ynt</u> y **gwynt** a'r **g**law?*
*Poni welwch-chwi'r **deri**'n ym**dar**aw?*
*Poni welwch-chwi'r **môr** yn **mer**win<u>aw</u>'r <u>tir</u>?*
*Poni welwch-chwi'r **g**<u>wir</u> yn ym**g**yweiriaw?*

[10] Dafydd Johnston, *Literature of Wales*, p. 33.

Each line demonstrates quite intense alliteration (highlighted here in **bold**), internal rhyme (<u>underlined</u>) and end rhyme (in roman). And in some cases the end rhyme serves also as an internal rhyme within the following line, e.g. *'ymdaraw'* at the end of the second line rhymes with *'glaw'* at the end of the first line, but also with *'merwinaw'* in the third line, and the last word of the third line, *'tir'*, rhymes internally with *'gwir'* in the middle of the fourth line!

But if Llywelyn's death inspired great poetry, it also placed the whole of the bardic tradition under threat. As the princes lost power, the poets lost their natural patrons and had to look to the gentry to find sponsors. And so this next age of poets is known as *Beirdd yr Uchelwyr* – poets of the gentry, and these poets had to travel from manor to mansion in order to earn a living.

The most outstanding of Welsh poets and one of the finest in all Europe was born in this period – Dafydd ap Gwilym. He learnt the craft of *cynghanedd* from his uncle who was constable at Newcastle Emlyn. Here is an extract from his famous poem *'Yr Wylan'* ('The Seagull'):

> *Yr wylan deg ar lanw, dioer*
> *Unlliw ag eiry neu wenlloer,*
> *Dilwch yw dy degwch di,*
> *Darn fel haul, dyrnfol heli.*
> *Ysgafn ar don eigion wyd,*
> *Esgudfalch edn bysgodfwyd.*
> *Yngo'r aud wrth yr angor*
> *Lawlaw â mi, lili môr.*
> *Llythr unwaith, llathr ei annwyd,*
> *Lleian ym mrig llanw môr wyd.*

> Truly, fair seagull on the tide,
> the colour of snow or the white moon,
> your beauty is without blemish,
> fragment like the sun, gauntlet of the salt.
> You are light on the ocean wave,
> swift, proud, fish-eating bird.
> There you'd go by the anchor
> hand in hand with me, sea lily.

Fashioned like a piece of shining paper,
you are a nun on the tide's crest.[11]

The *cynghanedd* in Dafydd ap Gwilym's poem is complete. Each
line reveals alliteration and internal rhyme in dense patterns that
will be explained more fully in the next chapter. But for now, as an
appetizer, let's consider the first and third line only.

If we divide the first line in two sections, we will see that the
consonants in section one are repeated in section two in exactly the
same order:

Yr wylan deg | ar lanw dioer
   r   l n d | r l n d   [12]

If, by contrast, we then divide the third line into three sections, we
will find that the first two sections rhyme together and that the
consonant at the beginning of the second section is the same as the
consonant at the beginning of the third section:

Dilwch | yw dy degwch | di.
  wch   d   wch d

And these are two of the patterns that form the rules of *cynghanedd*
as we still practise it today.

By this time, towards the beginning of the period of *Beirdd yr
Uchelwyr*, Einion Offeiriad (Einion the Priest) had further
formalized a grammar of *cerdd dafod*. The date generally ascribed
to his work is c.1320 and a version of his grammar can be seen in
Llyfr Coch Hergest ('The Red Book of Hergest'), housed today in
the Bodleian Library, Oxford. It is further believed that Dafydd
Ddu o Hiraddug edited the work in 1330 and that, in all probability,
Einion and Dafydd knew one another.

The next important landmark in the development of the code of
cerdd dafod is the 1451 Carmarthen eisteddfod. Dafydd Morgannwg
relates a fantastic tale about how this eisteddfod came about. He
describes how Llawdden Fardd, Vicar of Machynlleth, who came
originally from Llandeilo-Talybont in Glamorgan, went in 1450 to

---

[11] *Ibid*, p. 38.
[12] Note that 'y' and 'w' are vowels in the Welsh language – see Chapter 3.

Ystrad Tywi to visit Gruffydd ap Nicolas. During his stay a pauper calling himself a poet asked Llawdden to listen to a poem. It was so poor that Gruffydd and Llawdden decided that the practice of holding the eisteddfod would have to be reinstated in order to ensure the future of the ancient bardic tradition and restore self-respect to the art. Llawdden was convinced that a man of Gruffydd ap Nicolas's noble stature could persuade the king to agree to lift a ban that was allegedly on all eisteddfodau in this period. And indeed, the story goes on to claim that the reigning King, Henry the VI, agreed. Thus it came about that in 1451 Gruffydd ap Nicolas from Dinefwr sponsored a national eisteddfod in Carmarthen.

Whatever the background might be, it is true enough that an important eisteddfod was held in Carmarthen in 1451 and poets from the North and South flocked to the festival – one of whom was Dafydd ab Edmwnd. He further refined the code of *cerdd dafod* and introduced two new and complicated measures. He also won a silver chair at the eisteddfod for the best poem (and Dafydd Morgannwg claims that Llawdden was awarded a golden axe for the best handbook or essay on the different types of *cynghanedd*). Dafydd ap Edmwnd's changes weren't accepted immediately, and for a period there was some dispute as to which was the authorized code. However, over time, as prominent poets such as Tudur Aled tended to adhere to the new classification, it took root and became the basis of the code as practised today.

During the latter half of the fifteenth century other text books were produced, including those by Gwilym Tew and Gutun Owain. There can be little doubt that the aim of this rigorous classification was to narrow the circle of bards eligible to compete for the ever-dwindling pot of patronage!

A century or so later (in about 1570), Simwnt Fychan wrote his masterpiece *Pum Llyfr Cerddwriaeth* which lists the various degrees of poet-hood; the three main stages are as follows:

disgybl ysbâs heb radd	'unqualified apprentice'
disgybl disgyblaidd	'qualified apprentice'
pencerdd	'master poet'

The apprenticeship was almost entirely oral with virtually no written notes or lessons (which is exactly how the informal, pub-based circles learn to this day). In the old days however, would-be poets were required to have a thorough knowledge of many subject matters including the history and legends of the Brython people, a detailed knowledge of the Welsh language and a sound grasp of verse craft.

Sometimes the profession would run in families and the secrets of the craft passed on from father to son, but not always; at other times it seems that sons of master-poets would learn their craft from other poets and not necessarily from their fathers.

In the sixteenth century two important eisteddfodau were held at Caerwys (in 1523 and 1567) and each time the occasions were used to 'grade' or 'classify' the poets – according to the rules laid down by Dafydd ab Edmwnd.

And so it can be said that, after a millennium of development, the practice of *cynghanedd* was set.

About this time, also, poems that did not conform to the rules of *cynghanedd* began to become popular in Wales – and over the next five centuries or so, some of Wales's best poets, hymn writers perhaps in particular, turned to this kind of writing. The practice of *cynghanedd*, however, remained alive if not always in good health.

During the seventeenth century, poets still often addressed their muse to the nobility even though this was generally a nobility of the past and thus the tradition of passing on the rules of *cynghanedd* was upheld. The Phylip family of Ardudwy was particularly prominent in keeping the tradition at this time. They also carried on the tradition of *clera*[13] (where poets would wander from house to house) and indeed Siôn, the most prolific poet in the family, met an untimely death as he was drowned on the way home from one such *clera* expedition.

Amongst the many great eighteenth-century poets are Goronwy Owen and Ieuan Brydydd Hir. It was when I heard Goronwy Owen's elegy to his young daughter that I first became spellbound by *cynghanedd*. This is an extract from it:

> *Collais Elin liw hinon*
> *Fy ngeneth oleubleth Ion.*

> I lost Elin, the colour of sunshine,
> my fair-haired, joyful daughter.

---

[13] The term *clera* is particularly complex but it might be described as going on a circuit as a bard or minstrel soliciting gifts in return for poems and songs.

Here, as in the work of Dafydd ap Gwilym, we see an intricate pattern of internal rhyme (<u>underlined</u>) and alliteration (in **bold**) as well as an end rhyme (in roman). You can find the features in this next poem, taken from the work of Ieuan Brydydd Hir, *'Llys Ifor Hael'* ('The Hall of Ifor Hael'):

> *Llys Ifor hael, gwael yw'r gwedd, – yn garnau*
>   *Mewn gwerni mae'n gorwedd;*
> *Drain ac ysgall mall a'i medd,*
> *Mieri lle bu mawredd.*

A poor sight the hall of Ifor Hael – mounds
    In a swamp are lying,
    Thorn and blasted thistle own it,
    Bramble where was greatness.[14]

Nevertheless the most colourful figure in this period without doubt was Iolo Morganwg. As well as his own verse, his great contribution to Welsh poetry was his enthusiastic re-evaluation of the role of poets in Welsh cultural life. He established *Gorsedd Beirdd Ynys Prydain* (the bardic-druids' gathering) and organised its first meeting on Primrose Hill in London in 1792.[15] His *Cyfrinach Beirdd Ynys Prydain,* in which he deals extensively with *cerdd dafod*, was published posthumously.

By the nineteenth century the tradition of holding an annual eisteddfod was well established and *cynghanedd* had a prominent role to play in it. The competition requirements for a long poem (often longer than a thousand lines and sometimes over two thousand)[16] written in *cynghanedd* on such worthy subjects as *'Brawdoliaeth Gyffredinol'* ('Common Brotherhood') produced dozens of long-winded pieces. As late as 1891 compositions of over one thousand lines were common, until in 1896 a rule was introduced which restricted poems to no more than six hundred lines!

Although the 1800s are considered by some a low point in the

---

[14] *Welsh Verse*, Tony Conran, p. 238.
[15] For a thorough introduction to the history of the eisteddfod, see Hywel Teifi Edwards, *The Eisteddfod (Writers of Wales series),* Cardiff (1990).
[16] Cf. *Yr Atgyfodiad,* 'The Resurrection', Ieuan Glan Geirionydd (1850).

history of the craft of *cynghanedd*, they did produce a number of beautiful and lasting poems. One such example is the sensitive elegy by Robert ap Gwilym Ddu where we can hear how *cynghanedd* helps to express the sense of grief at the loss of his daughter.

Awdl Goffa am ei Ferch

*Ymhol<u>ais</u>, cr*wydr<u>ais</u> mewn cr*i; – o*ch alar!*
*Hir ch*wiliais amdan*i;*
Chwilio'r cell<u>oedd</u> <u>oedd</u> e<u>idd</u>i,
*A ch*wilio heb ei ch*ael h*i.*

By the twentieth century the National Eisteddfod had grown into an elaborate cultural event with many competitions ranging from baritone solos to knitting socks! However, it is probably fair to say that the high point of this itinerant and unique cultural festival has always been the ceremony of the 'Chairing of the Bard' – so called because in it the poet of the winning composition is awarded a grand chair.

There are two main poetry prizes in the National Eisteddfod of today – the Crown and the Chair – and while the Crown is awarded for a poem not written in *cynghanedd*, to win the Chair, the work must be composed entirely within the rules of the 'strict metres'. We have already touched upon the practice of awarding the Chair to the poet of the winning competition. The poets of kings and princes were held in high esteem by their benefactors and thus had their own Chair in the courts and palaces. The poet would accompany his patrons at wars and battles, he would entertain his family, he would sit with him at banquets and he would compose works complimenting his estate, his generosity, bravery and wisdom. One of the ways that the kings and princes would repay the bard's loyalty was by awarding a prize whose importance was clear to all their subjects, namely a chair that was only surpassed by the throne itself.

The days when we had our own kings and princes in Wales have long gone, but the accolade paid to a poet immersed in the noble art of *cynghanedd* has remained. Since the latter half of the nineteenth century, the Chair in the National Eisteddfod has been awarded to poets for an extended composition, known as an *awdl*. Upon winning the Chair in the National Eisteddfod one gains the title *Prifardd*, which literally means 'Chief Poet'. As already mentioned, in the early years the *awdl* could extend to many hundreds of lines, and although they were in *cynghanedd*, the artistry of poetry was sometimes lacking. At the turn of the twentieth century, however, *cynghanedd* broke new ground when T. Gwynn Jones won the Chair with his *awdl* on the subject *'Ymadawiad Arthur'* ('The Passing of Arthur'). In this poem the lines flow from one into the other with outstanding grace and clarity. It is also significantly shorter than previous attempts as it stands at under five hundred lines and in more recent years the competition usually asks for a work of no more than two or three hundred lines.

Important as the Chair is, it is by no means the only competition open to *cynganeddwyr* (the practitioners of *cynghanedd*) in the National Eisteddfod. There are competitions for shorter poems each day, and every year one of the most popular venues on the *Maes* ('eisteddfod field') is *Y Babell Lên* ('literary pavilion'). Hundreds of *cynghanedd* fans pack the tent every day, eagerly awaiting what is known as *Ymryson y Beirdd* (literally 'battle of the bards'), which is a literary competition like no other. Queues form outside the tent more than an hour beforehand, and it has been said, on some occasions, that there have been more people in the *Babell Lên* than in the main arena.

Teams of poets from across the whole of Wales battle against each other throughout the week to reach the final, and the winners of this receive the coveted trophy – *Tlws Rolant o Fôn*. In every round, there are three teams of four poets, representing different areas of Wales. There is also an adjudicator. R. J. Rowlands, a poet and journalist from Caernarfon, became such a renowned adjudicator of *Ymryson y Beirdd* that his bardic name 'Meuryn' is now the official title for all adjudicators of such competitions. Indeed, even the Welsh verb 'to adjudicate' in this context has developed from his bardic name, and is known as *'meuryna'*. The *Meuryn* is always a highly respected poet with in-depth knowledge of the rules of *cynghanedd*. He gives marks out of ten to every poet for his or her composition. There are two aspects of this competition that set it apart. Firstly, each composition has to be in *cynghanedd*. If the *Meuryn* spots a transgression of the rules, he issues a severe and shameful public reprimand. The second aspect fills each competitor with even more trepidation than the first. Each poet has only twenty minutes in which to complete the composition!

At the beginning of the *Ymryson*, the three teams appear on stage, pens and paper at the ready. The *Meuryn* announces the different tasks. The audience is then entertained while the poets disappear backstage for their frenzy of composition. When the twenty minutes are up, the teams are summoned back to the stage. Some of the tasks might not be quite finished. They beg for mercy. None is shown. They have to appear on stage. The audience is waiting. But somehow when the time comes to stand in front of the microphone, the *cynghanedd* has invariably worked its magic. The poet has a composition ready to declaim, and the audience is mesmerized. The whole hour is televised live and uncensored and transmitted that very night. It is one of the most watched events of the whole National Eisteddfod.

The National Eisteddfod however lasts for only one week at the beginning of August each year. During the rest of the year, one of the most popular programmes on Radio Cymru, the Welsh language channel, is *Talwrn y Beirdd* ('The Bardic Cockpit'), but here, unlike the National Eisteddfod, the teams have a week to prepare, and some of the tasks do not require *cynghanedd*. These national showcases rest on a basis of local activity that takes place in pubs, village halls and chapel vestries, where competitions and poetry readings provide popular entertainment. A variation on the theme is the less formal *stomp*. This is a competition that dispenses with the *Meuryn* and lets the audience decide the winner – by popular acclaim. That fortunate favourite is honoured with a stool, not a chair!

Cynghanedd may be oral and aural, but it has a voice in print too in *Barddas*, a quarterly publication devoted to *cerdd dafod* with a circulation of almost a thousand, which makes it the second highest-selling poetry magazine in the UK. Then there is the *Cyfansoddiadau*, which is the collection of the winning entries of the National Eisteddfod, together with the adjudications – some two hundred and fifty pages in all. This publication is eagerly awaited each year and sells some 6,000 copies within a couple of weeks. To give the reader a sense of proportion, a quick multiplication of these figures with the number of Welsh speakers compared with the number of English speakers in Britain alone, suggests that the *Barddas* sale is comparable to an English poetry journal selling 100,000 copies in Britain alone, and an equivalent to the *Cyfansoddiadau* selling 600,000. Which publishing house in London would not turn green with envy at such potential? And remember, these are figures for copies sold, not copies read! To this must be added the fact that, in this age of Information Technology, the ancient craft has its own website called simply 'cynghanedd.com'.

A fairly recent development is the annual *Gŵyl Gynganeddu*, a weekend-long festival held in Tŷ Newydd, the writers' centre in Cricieth, Gwynedd. Here performances, workshops and debates attract a passionate gathering of poets, participants and listeners from all generations.

And so we see that while we might not know the birthday of *cynghanedd*, we can be certain that it is still enjoying a very full and active life.

CHAPTER 3

Four Parts of the Harmony

The craft of *cynghanedd* enables poets in Wales to create a work of art by bringing sound and substance together in a beautiful and unique way. As such, and as has been suggested already, it is something to be spoken and heard. This chapter, which begins to explain the four basic types of *cynghanedd*, must therefore be read aloud at least in part.

To compose *cynghanedd* we must be able to identify 'stress'. This is the most important aspect of learning the craft. But before we can tackle this, we need to reconsider what constitutes rhyme, because this is different in the Welsh language from elsewhere – and from English in particular.

Consider the simplest nursery rhyme:

> *Mary, Mary* quite *contrary*
> how does your garden <u>grow</u>
> with silver **bells**
> and cockle **shells**
> and pretty maids all in a <u>row</u>.

The <u>underlined</u> words rhyme together and similarly those in **bold**, and those in *italics*. Where the rhyming words are a pair of monosyllables, the vowel and final consonant(s) are identical – e.g. b**ells**, sh**ells**. Where the rhyming words have more than one syllable, the final two vowels and consonant(s) are often identical – e.g. **Mary**, contr**ary**. This is the standard rhyming pattern in English verse. In Welsh verse however, a match in the final vowel alone can constitute a rhyme – no matter how many syllables the word might have – because that vowel is always clearly enunciated. Thus a word such as *cysgu* ('to sleep') may rhyme with *dysgu* ('to learn'), where both syllables rhyme, but also with *canu* ('to sing') and *du* ('black'), which rhyme only with the final syllable of the first word. Similarly *bychan* ('small') may rhyme with *dychan* ('satire') but also with *baban* ('baby') and *tan* ('until') or indeed *tân* ('fire'), where '*a*' and '*â*' are vowels of different lengths.

Along with rhyme, a traditional characteristic of the special sound
of poetry is alliteration. Take these two lines from Tennyson's 'The
splendour falls on castle walls' where the matching consonants
which together create alliteration have been noted in bold:

> And **s**nowy **s**ummits old in **s**tory:
> The **l**ong **l**ight shakes across the **l**akes

Lastly there is rhythm, and within the concept of 'rhythm' one can
talk of 'stress', which brings us to the very first lesson on how to
compose a line of *cynghanedd*.

3.1 Stress

Readers will be well aware of the role of a regular rhythm in many
poems, and many anthologies of English poetry begin with an
introduction to the difference between the various rhythmic
patterns. The most common are the following four:

the iambus	(– /)	'I saw three ships come sailing in';
the trochee	(/ –)	'Incy-Wincy Spider;
the anapaest	(– – /)	'When I go to the garden the roses aren't there';
the dactyl	(/ – –)	'Merrily, merrily shall I live now'.

Quite often, such examples are accompanied with the appropriate
ti-tum, tum-ti, ti-ti-tum and tum-ti-ti chants – where 'tum' (as ' / ')
denotes the stressed syllable! This is the metrical form of the poem
that we can measure in order to identify a recurrent pattern of
stressed and unstressed syllables.

In *cynghanedd*, stress is the most important characteristic of all,
but not primarily in order to form a regular rhythmic pattern as
above. Indeed lines of *cynghanedd* don't necessarily have regular
rhythmic patterns – though they observe a beat or pulse. Just like
music.

Think of a piece of music written in ¾ time. Each bar might well
have a different rhythm, perhaps a dotted minim, perhaps a minim
and a crotchet, perhaps a triplet followed by two crotchets, perhaps
six quavers. But each bar will observe the ¾ pulse and the music
will flow accordingly from one bar to the next.

Compare:

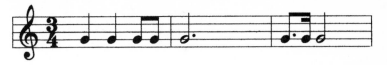

with:

The second example has a regular recurring rhythm while the first does not. Yet both examples have a ¾ pulse. Lines of *cynghanedd* flow like the music in the first example – their rhythmic pattern is unpredictable but they have a certain beat that holds the music together.

Yet I maintain that in order to be able to write *cynghanedd*, we must be able to hear exactly where the stress lies in each word. Let's see if we can do this and then I shall explain why!

Now, unlike English, Welsh is a heavily stressed language. Like Italian and Spanish, Welsh words have an accent of intensity on one syllable that gives the language its well-known lilt. Where a word has more than one syllable, this accent lies, more often than not, on the penultimate syllable.

In order to identify the stress, I find it useful to ask students to stand and bend their knees to indicate that they hear the stressed part of the phrase or word. But as it is not always practical to stand up and down when trying to compose *cynghanedd*, then a simple '/' can be inserted as shorthand to show the exact location of this stress.

Let's start by observing the stress in some place names in Wales:

/
Caerfyrddin

/
Aberaeron

/
Eifionydd

/
Llanelli

/
Y Bari

/
Gwynedd

/
Meifod

/
Pwll

/
Rhyl

/
Caerdydd

/
Abergwaun

/
Aberdâr

(The last three place names have been deliberately included as exceptions to prove the rule – as they do not carry the stress on the penultimate syllable!)

The next step is to realise that when words are put together, the stress of the first words in the group yield their weight to the stress in the final word. This becomes the main stress of the phrase.

Let's see what happens when we add to the above place names phrases such as:

/ /
mynd i – 'to go to';

/ /
dod o – 'to come from';

/– /
aros yn – 'to stay in'.

/
Mynd i Aberaeron

/
Mynd i'r Rhyl

/
Dod o Abergwaun

/
Dod o Eifionydd

/
Aros yn Y Bari

/
Aros yn Aberdâr

And so while each separate word will have its own stress, there will always be one stress that overrules the others when words are put together. The overruling stress will be found towards the end of the phrase – either on the ultimate, or penultimate syllable.

Once the stress has been identified we can start to find *cynghanedd*. In other words, we can begin to 'harmonize' the words.

/
Take a word such as CARIAD ('love').

The stress falls on the first vowel '*a*' – which forms the penultimate syllable '*car*'. (It also happens to be the first syllable, but it will be easier to think of it as the last-but-one).

/   –
CARIAD

Imagine a simple X-ray photograph of the human leg. It reveals nothing but bones. Everything else, from the skin and muscles to the veins, has disappeared. If we take an 'X-ray photograph' of the word CARIAD, and take away all the vowels leaving only the bare bones of the consonants before and after the stress (as well as the / to denote the stress itself), we will see the following 'skeleton' or 'pattern':

C / R

This is the pattern that will form the heart of our harmony.

In order to find words that are in harmony with CARIAD, we must simply search for words that have the very same skeleton, i.e. the same consonants around the stressed syllable. e.g:

CURO ('to beat') C / R;

CÔR ('choir') C / R;

CORRACH ('dwarf') C / R.

(Note that the consonant after the unstressed syllable should not be the same).

Words such as CREU ('to create') or CREDU ('to believe') are not in harmony with CARIAD, for even though they both contain the consonants 'C' and 'R', the stress does not lie between these two consonants.

In CREU, the stress lies *after* C and R: CR /.

In CREDU the stress lies *between* R and D, i.e. *after* the C and R again – CR / D.

Since the location of the stress is an integral part of the word's skeletal pattern, CARIAD is not in *cynghanedd* with either CREU or CREDU. CR / and CR / D is not the same pattern as C / R!

In the case of two monosyllabic words, in order to harmonize these we only need to match the consonants immediately **before** the stress in both words e.g.

CAR ('car') is in harmony with COF ('memory')

and CI ('dog'), since each subscribes to the C / pattern.

Now that we have learnt why stress is important, let's practise how to identify different words with similar skeletons.

Exercise 1

Which of the following words belong to the beams of the stars below?

a) SIR   ('county')
   SEREN   ('star')
   STRYD   ('street')
   SIRIOL   ('cheerful')
   SIŴR   ('sure')
   SIARADUS   ('talkative')
   SAWR   ('smell')
   SAER   ('carpenter')

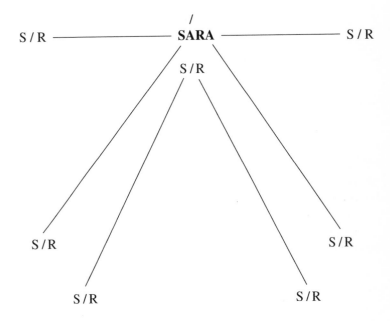

TIP
Begin by identifying the stress, then work out the 'X-ray photograph' or pattern in each word. Note: to make life a little simpler, the words in this exercise have been carefully chosen so that, where there is more than one syllable, the stress in each is on the penultimate syllable!

b) DWYLO   ('hands')
   DYLANWAD   ('influence')
   DWL   ('silly')
   DOLI   ('dolly')
   ADEILAD   ('building')
   ODLI   ('to rhyme')

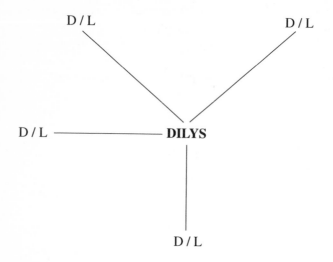

c) PÊL   ('ball')
   PAWB   ('everybody')
   POLYN   ('pole')
   PYLU   ('to fade')
   PÔS   ('puzzle')
   PWYLAIDD   ('Polish')

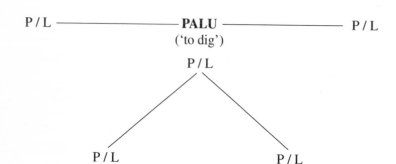

3.2 Four types of *Cynghanedd*

Now that we can hear the stress and harmonize individual words, we need some understanding of the Welsh alphabet before we can attempt to learn the next step.

In the Welsh language there are seven vowels – *A E I O U W Y.*

We also have extra consonants that, to the untrained eye, might appear as two consonants joined together:

Dd	pronounced as 'th' in 'the'
Ff	pronounced as 'f' in 'friend' –
	(in Welsh a single 'f' is pronounced as 'v' as in 'very')
Ng	pronounced as 'ng' in 'singing'
Ll	has no real approximations in English
Rh	has no real approximations in English

We also have *Ch Th* and *Ph* as in English, but *Ch* is pronounced as 'ch' in 'loch' and not 'chair'; and *Th* as 'th' in 'thistle' not 'the'. To this we must add that '*h*' sometimes behaves as a consonant, sometimes as a vowel.

Bearing this in mind, we can now turn our attention to the four basic types of *cynghanedd*, known as:

Cynghanedd Groes;[1]

Cynghanedd Draws;

Cynghanedd Sain;

Cynghanedd Lusg.

These terms have been nicely translated by Idwal Lloyd who coined the following descriptions: 'The Criss-Cross Harmony' for *Cynghanedd Groes*, 'The Bridging Harmony' for *Cynghanedd*

---

[1] Throughout this next chapter, readers who have not yet learnt Welsh might notice that the first letter of some of the Welsh words changes from time to time. This is in accordance with the rules of Welsh grammar, which demand that letters 'mutate' to clarify the role of the word in the sentence. The best policy for the purposes of this exercise is to accept that *Croes* sometimes appears as *Groes* and *Llusg* sometimes as *Lusg*.

Draws, 'The Sonorous Harmony' for *Cynghanedd Sain* and 'The Echoing Harmony' for *Cynghanedd Lusg*.

In the first two types listed – *Croes* and *Draws* – the line is split into two, with two important stresses and a match, or balance, between the consonants in both sections. (To continue with the references to music, it might be helpful to consider these sections as two 'bars' and the caesura or break between the two as a 'bar line'.) In the third type of *cynghanedd* – *Sain* – the line is split into three bars. Between the first two there is an internal rhyme and between the last two there is a consonantal balance. The fourth – *Llusg* – is split into two bars bound together by rhyme only.

The length of a line of *cynghanedd* can vary from a short four-syllable line to an impressive sixteen-syllable line. However, the most common length by far is a seven-syllable line and on the whole, the examples listed below will be seven syllables long.

3.3 *Cynghanedd Groes*

Once upon a time there was a young man who was passionately in love with a beautiful woman called Meri Jên. Though he had sent her flowers and chocolates and cards of all description, she seemed not to notice him, until one day he decided to write her a line of *cynghanedd*. He thought long and hard about the compliment he would pay her and finally decided to compare her to the most delicious thing he had ever eaten. This was jam! He loved the taste of jam. Now, he realised that his love for Meri Jên was far greater than the small spoonful of jam he used to spread on his morning toast. In fact, his love for Meri was at least as great and as deep as the ocean. This thought gave him the inspiration he needed to compose the following line which, you will be glad to learn, captured Meri's heart!

Môr o jam yw Meri Jên.

The line has two bars

$$/ \qquad\qquad\qquad /$$
Môr o jam | yw Meri Jên.

Môr ('sea')
o ('of')
yw ('is')

'Mary Jane is a sea of jam!'

The stress in the first bar falls on '*jam*' and in the second on '*Jên*'. (As both the stressed words are monosyllables we need only note consonants before the stress in our harmony. Remember the example of *Car*, *Cof* and *Ci* above.)

The X-ray photograph of the first bar reveals the pattern:

m r j /

and the X-ray photograph of the second bar reveals an identical pattern:

m r j /.

Both bars are thus in complete harmony. The balance between the consonants is perfect. This, therefore, is an example of a line of *Cynghanedd Groes*.

Let's now look at three more examples of *Cynghanedd Groes*, and in so doing look carefully at the stress pattern of the word immediately before the caesura (the 'bar line') and the word at the very end of the line in each example:

(i)   **Hynaf oll heno wyf i**   (Guto'r Glyn '*I Ddafydd ab Ieuan – Abad Glyn Egwestl*' 15th Century)

Hynaf oll ('oldest of them all')
heno ('tonight')
wyf i ('am I')

'Tonight, I am the oldest of them all'

        /   /
Hynaf oll I heno wyf i
h n f / I h n   f /

(ii)   **Darn o'r haul draw yn rhywle**   (Dic Jones '*Miserere*'
                                                  20th Century)

    Darn ('a part')
    o'r haul ('of the sun')
    draw ('over there')
    yn rhywle ('somewhere')

'Over there, somewhere, a part of the sun'.

       /   /
Darn o'r haul | draw yn rhywle
d rn   r h/ | | dr   n rh/ |

(iii)   **Dienw yw dy wyneb**   (Alun Jones '*Enwogrwydd*'
                                                  20th Century)

    Dienw ('nameless')
    yw ('is')
    dy ('your')
    wyneb ('face')

'Yours is a nameless face'

    /   /
Dienw | yw dy wyneb
d /n | d   / n

Did you notice the stress pattern in each example?

In the first example:

       /   /
Hynaf oll | heno wyf i

there is a stress on the last syllable immediately before the caesura and a stress on the last syllable of the line.

In the second example:

      /   / –
Darn o'r haul | draw yn rhywle

there is a stress on the last syllable immediately before the caesura and a stress on the penultimate syllable of the line where '–' represents an unstressed syllable.

In the third example:

$$/ \quad - \qquad\quad / \quad -$$
Dienw | yw dy wyneb

there is a stress on the penultimate syllable before the caesura and a stress on the penultimate syllable of the line.

These three examples represent the only three possible variations of stress pattern in a line of *Cynghanedd Groes* (and indeed *Cynghanedd Draws* which you will meet in section 3.4).

The missing pattern here is:

$$/ \ - \ | \quad /$$

as it is not considered harmonious to have the first part of the line ending with the stress on the penultimate syllable and the second part of the line with the stress on the last syllable.

Exercise 2

Here are the beginnings of four lines of *Cynghanedd Groes*. Below them you will find the phrases needed to complete the lines, but they have been jumbled up. Remember, each bar will have the same pattern or skeleton, which must include the consonants as well as the stress. So start by identifying the stress in the missing lines, and then identify the pattern of stress and consonants.

> **TIP**
> *Together the syllables in each line add up to 7!*

$$/$$
Un awr harddach   ('a more beautiful hour')
r h /rdd

(Dic Jones '*Ar ei Chanfed Pen-blwydd*' 20th C)

/
A mi'n fawr   ('as I am tall')
  m n f / r
                                   (Alan Llwyd *'Clychau'r Gog 1987'*
                                   20th C)

/
Roedd eira   ('there was snow')
r   dd / r
                                   (Alan Llwyd 'Taid' 20th C)

/
A breuddwyd   ('and a dream')
  br / dd
                                   (Guto'r Glyn *'Ateb i Lywelyn ap
                                   Gutun'* 15th C)

ar y dderwen   ('on the oak tree')

y mae'n fyrrach   ('it is shorter')

na'r hwyrddydd   ('than the evening')

heb arwyddion   ('without signs')

3.4 *Cynghanedd Draws*

Right in the very most western corner of north Pembrokeshire there lived a fierce giant long, long ago. His name was Ysbaddaden Bencawr. He would sit for hours in his giant's seat on top of Garn Bristgarn to observe the world beneath him. When Culhwch came to ask him for the hand of Olwen, his beautiful daughter, he was enraged... The story of Culhwch's pursuit of Ysbaddaden's daughter is wonderful and well worth learning, but alas it is too long as a preface for this exercise. For now, I shall report to you only one line from the exchange that took place between Ysbaddaden and Culhwch when they first met. The fierce old giant roared:

    A chei FYTH law fy merch fach!

And this is an example of *Cynghanedd Draws*!

The line has two bars:

     /   /
A chei FYTH | law fy merch fach

A chei ('and you shall have')
FYTH ('NEVER')
law ('the hand')
fy merch ('of my daughter')
fach ('little')

'And you shall never have my little daughter's hand!'

The stress in the first bar falls on *'fyth'* and in the second on *'fach'*.

The X-ray photograph of the first bar reveals the pattern

    ch f /

and the X-ray photograph of the second bar reveals the following pattern:

    l f m r ch f /

You will notice immediately that there is a significant difference between the two bars and that the balance between the consonants is less than perfect.

But let's take a closer look. Remember that the term *Cynghanedd Draws* can be translated as the 'Bridging Harmony'. Let's therefore build a bridge over the first part of the second bar – over the letters *'l f m'* and *'r'*. We are left with the pattern *'ch f /'*, which is the core of the line as it includes the stressed syllable.

Once the bridge is in place, we can cross over from the first bar, over the beginning of the second, to the stress.

We then find a consonantal balance between the two bars:

    ch f / and (l f m r) ch f /

Some might think that the *Cynghanedd Draws* is a diluted form of the *Cynghanedd Groes*. This misses the point. The softer nature of the *Cynghanedd Draws* is beautiful and resonant. It plays an important role in lending poems written in *cynghanedd* a smooth expression as the line trips lightly over the bridge to the stressed syllable on the other side.

Some more examples:

(i) **Yn llawen iawn mewn llwyn ir**   (Dafydd ap Gwilym
                                          '*Cyngor y Biogen*' 14ᵗʰ C)

Yn llawen ('joyful')
iawn ('very')
mewn ('in')
llwyn ('grove')
ir ('green')

'Very joyful in the green grove'

```
        /                    /
Yn llawen iawn | mewn llwyn ir
 n ll    n   /  |(m)  n ll   n /
```

(ii) **Mae ynom, bawb, ddymuniad**   (Dic Jones '*Cefn Gwlad*'
                                          20ᵗʰ C)

Mae ('there is')
ynom ('within us')
bawb ('all')
ddymuniad ('a wish')

'Within each one of us there is a longing'

```
      /                   /
Mae ynom | bawb ddymuniad
 m  / n  |(b   b dd) m/n
```

(iii) **I fyw yn glos wrth gefn gwlad**   (Dic Jones '*Cefn Gwlad*'
                                            20ᵗʰ C)

I fyw ('to live')
yn glos ('close')
wrth ('to')
gefn gwlad ('the country')

'To live close to nature'

```
        /                   /
I fyw yn glos | wrth gefn gwlad
 f    n gl/   |(rth  g) fn g  l/
```

Exercise 3

Here are the beginnings of four lines of *Cynghanedd Draws*. Below
the phrases needed to complete the lines are jumbled up.
Remember, you must match the same pattern or skeleton . . . and
together the syllables in each line add up to seven!

/
Eiliadau | ('seconds')
 l / d

          (Alan Llwyd *'Clychau'r Gog'* 20th C)

     /
Awyr goch | ('a red sky')
  r g /

          (Alan Llwyd *'Hwyrddydd'* 20th C)

   /
Os ydwyf | ('if I am')
 s / d

          (Meirion MacIntyre Huws *'Côt'* 20th C)

    /
yma nawr | ('here now')
  m n /

          (Tudur Dylan Jones *'Ar y We'* 21st C)

yng nghwmni neb   ('in nobody's company')

yw pob blodyn   ('is each flower')

yn drwsiadus   ('dapper, neat and tidy')

yn friwiau i gyd   ('full of bruises')

3.5 *Cynghanedd Sain*

Dewi Emrys is one of those legendary and colourful figures in our poetic tradition. He was born in Ceredigion in 1881 and brought up in Rhosycaerau, North Pembrokeshire. A trained journalist, he was later ordained as a minister with the Presbyterian Church, but in 1918 he returned to journalism and led what is often described as a 'Bohemian' life in London. Eventually he came back to Wales, to Talgarreg, where he died in 1952. He won the National Eisteddfod Crown in 1926 and the Chair no fewer than four times. (Since then it has become a rule that any one poet is only allowed to win both the Chair and the Crown twice!) For an eisteddfod in Colwyn Bay in 1947 he wrote two *englynion*[2] to the Horizon. Dewi Emrys himself is said to have believed that the *englyn* that didn't win was the better. Be that as it may, his second choice took the first prize and soon became a favourite throughout Wales.

> *Wele rith fel ymyl rhod – o'n cwmpas*
> *Campwaith dewin hynod,*
> *Hen linell bell nad yw'n bod*
> *Hen derfyn nad yw'n darfod.*

The third line of this *englyn* is an example of *Cynghanedd Sain*:

Hen linell bell nad yw'n bod.

Unlike the lines of Cynghanedd Groes and Draws, this line has three bars:

Hen linell | bell | nad yw'n bod

Hen linell ('an old line')
bell ('faraway')
nad yw'n bod ('that does not exist')

'An old line faraway that doesn't exist'

---

[2] An *englyn* is a four-lined stanza in *cynghanedd* which we will meet in the next chapter.

The last word in the first bar rhymes with the last word in the second bar (which, in this case, happens to be the only word!)

Hen linell | bell
       ell   *ell*

The stress in the second bar falls on '*bell*' and in the third bar on '*bod*'.

The X-ray photograph of the second and third bars reveals this pattern:

   /   /
bell | nad yw'n bod
b/ | n d   n b/

Using the technique of crossing via the the bridge learnt in the section on the *Cynghanedd Draws* above, we see that the pattern immediately around the stress is the same in both bars – the consonants are in balance.

b / | (n d n) b /

The three bars are in perfect harmony. A rhyme binds bars one and two and a consonantal balance binds bars two and three.

        /   /
Hen linell | bell | nad yw'n bod
    ell   *ell*
        b/ (n d   n) b/

In the examples below, it will become clear that the consonantal balance between bars 2 and 3 in *Cynghanedd Sain* is less strict than in *Cynghanedd Groes* or *Draws*. It is only the consonant *immediately before* the stress that needs to find a match on the other side. The ones after it can be ignored and we can cross over consonants in both the middle and the last section – as long as there is a match immediately before the stress:

(i)   **Un pnawn llawn pelydrau llwch**   (Ceri Wyn Jones
     '*Cymwynaswr*' 20th C)

Un pnawn ('one afternoon')
llawn ('full of')
pelydrau ('beams/ rays')
llwch ('dust')

'One afternoon full of dust beams'

```
     /          /                    /
Un pnawn | llawn | pelydrau llwch
    awn     awn
          ll /   |(p | dr)   ll /
```

(ii)   **Yng ngaeaf diwethaf ein dydd**   (Gerallt Lloyd Owen
     '*Gwenoliaid*' 20th C)

Yng ngaeaf ('in the winter')
diwethaf ('last')
ein ('our')
dydd ('day')

'In the last winter of our day'.

```
      /            /                 /
Yng ngaeaf | diwethaf | ein dydd
      af          af
          d  /          (n)d  /
```

(iii)   **At ddŵr rhyw harbwr o hyd**   (Twm Morys '*Dod
Adre*' 21st C)

At ('towards')
ddŵr ('water')
rhyw ('some')
harbwr ('harbour')
o hyd ('always')

'Always towards some harbour's water'

```
     /              /           /
At ddŵr | rhyw harbwr | o hyd
    wr            wr
       (r)     h /            h /
```

Exercise 4

Here are the beginnings of four lines of *Cynghanedd Sain*. Below them the phrases needed to complete the lines are jumbled up. Remember, you must match the same pattern or skeleton . . . and together the syllables in each line add up to seven! Only this time, of course, you need to find TWO missing bars and you will need to pay careful attention to the meanings of the phrases as well as the *cynghanedd* to get this exercise right!

Ac fe ddaeth | ('and he came')
  aeth |

                          (Iwan Llwyd '*Y Barcud Ola*' 21ˢᵗ C)

Y gwarth a'r trais | ('the disgrace and violence')
  ais |

                          (Myrddin ap Dafydd '*Newid Enw*' 21ˢᵗ C)

Ar draws gwlad | ('cross country')
  ad |

                          (Idris Reynolds '*Dyletswydd*' 20ᵗʰ C)

Rwy'n galw | ('I call')
  w | (Tudur Dylan Jones '*Y Môr*' 20ᵗʰ C)

yn gaeth   ('imprisoned')

di   ('you')

deimlaist   ('you felt')

hi   ('hers')

du   ('black')

ei henw   ('her name')

mewn dillad   ('in clothes')

a gwan   ('and weak')

3.6 *Cynghanedd Lusg*

You will recall that in years gone by, the Chair at the National Eisteddfod used to be awarded for compositions in *cynghanedd* that were thousands of lines long. In more recent years, the number of lines has been limited to somewhere between two and three hundred. But in 1975 Gerallt Lloyd Owen, under the pseudonym 'Bronwydd', won the Chair to great acclaim for an *awdl* of no more than some hundred and fifty lines long, which proves that quality is always more important than quantity. His remarkable composition enchants the reader from beginning to end, and starts with a form of *cynghanedd* often described as the simplest of all – namely *Cynghanedd Lusg*.

In each of the three types of *cynghanedd* already discussed, there has been a need to balance consonants to a greater or lesser degree. In the *Cynghanedd Lusg*, there is no need to worry about consonants at all, as the only element that needs to be balanced is an internal rhyme between the last syllable in the first bar and the stressed syllable of the second bar – which, in a line of *Cynghanedd Lusg,* will always be the penultimate syllable. So here again, we see that observing the main stresses of the line is all-important.

Listen to how Gerallt Lloyd Owen opens his *awdl 'Yr Afon'* ('The River'):

> **Pan feddwn dalent plentyn**
> **I weld llais a chlywed llun**
>
> When I possessed the child's gift
> To see a voice and hear a picture

You will recognise the pattern in the second line as an example of *Cynghanedd Draws* where we cross over the unmatched '*ch*' in the middle:

>   /   /
> **I weld llais | a chlywed llun**
>   ld ll / | (ch)l   d ll /

But let's examine the first line.

It has two bars:

Pan feddwn dalent I plentyn

Pan ('when')
feddwn ('I possessed')
dalent ('the gift')
plentyn ('of the child')

The last syllable of the first bar gives us the sound '*ent*' – this is the sound that needs to be rhymed in the stressed part of the second bar. (Note that there are no hard and fast rules about the position of the caesura and the lines can be divided in many places. This helps to give *cynghanedd* its fluidity. Here the caesura comes very late in the line as the two most important words are '*dalent*' and '*plentyn*'.)

The stress in the second bar falls on the penultimate syllable of the last word:

/   /

plentyn (ent)

/   /

Pan feddwn dal*ent* I pl*ent*yn
ent I   *ent*

This internal rhyme forms an 'echo' between the bars and makes the line an example of *Cynghanedd Lusg*.

Here are some more examples, and you will find that in the *Cynghanedd Lusg*, the stress in the second bar **always** falls on the penultimate syllable; i.e. a line of *Cynghanedd Lusg* will never end with a word that carries the stress on the final syllable.

(i)   **Mae arch yn Ystrad Marchell**   (Guto'r Glyn '*Marwnad Llywelyn ab y Moel*' 15th C)

Mae ('there is')
arch ('a coffin')
yn ('in')
Ystrad Marchell ('Ystrad Marchell')

'There is a coffin in Ystrad Marchell'

/   /

Mae *arch* I yn Ystrad M*arch*ell
arch I   *arch*

(ii) **Afal pêr ac aderyn**   (Lewis Glyn Cothi
                                            '*Marwnad Siôn y Glyn*'
                                            15th C)

        Afal ('apple')
        pêr ('sweet')
        ac ('and')
        aderyn ('bird')

        'a sweet apple and a bird'

               /   /
        Afal pêr| **ac ad*er*yn**
             er| *er*

(iii) **Yno'r es am un rheswm**   (Tudur Dylan Jones
                                            '*Medi 18, 1997*' 20th C)

        Yno ('there')
        es ('I went')
        am ('for')
        un ('one')
        rheswm ('reason')

        'I went there for one reason'

               /   /
        Yno'r *es*| am un rh*es*wm
             es| *es*

Exercise 5

Here are the beginnings of four lines of *Cynghanedd Lusg*. Below
them the phrases needed to complete the lines are jumbled up.
Remember you must simply match the rhyme in the syllable at the
end of the first bar with the rhyme in the penultimate syllable in the
second bar . . . and together the syllables in each line add up to
seven!

        Heb amserlen | ('without a timetable')
                  en
                                     (Idris Reynolds '*Trên*' 20th C)

Lladd hyder |
  er

('the killing of confidence')

(Tony Elliot '*Llwyddiant y Sais 1282–1980*' 20th C)

Mor dawel |
  el

('so quiet')

(T. Gwynn Jones '*Y Breuddwyd*' 20th C)

Ond cyn bedd |
  edd

('but before the grave')

(Goronwy Owen '*Gwahodd*' 18th C)

na threnau

('nor trains')

dyma 'ngweddi

('this is my prayer')

oedd Llywelyn

('was Llywelyn')

yng Nghilmeri

('in Cilmeri')

CHAPTER 4

Tolerated Transgressions

I have already noted my dislike of the term 'strict metre' often used in English to describe *cynghanedd*. The word 'strict' is so severe.

It is too easy to become obsessed with the rules of *cynghanedd* and to forget that they serve a purpose, namely to help the writer compose beautiful lines, lines that sing. As I said in the introduction to this handbook, practising the basic skills and learning the theory is a liberating process, not a restrictive one.

It is true that some rules in *cynghanedd* must never be broken. Take stress, for example. When the rules of stress are ignored the line can never be described as *cynghanedd* because a discordant sound which jars the ear is produced. However, things are not always as 'strict' as they seem, and in this next section I shall note some of the transgressions from the patterns described above that are tolerated in certain circumstances.

4.1 This is Where the Fun Begins!

(i) the letter 'h'

As in French, the letter '*h*' in Welsh can sometimes count as a vowel. As such it does not always need to be weighed when we balance the consonants.

The following line is thus a perfectly acceptable example of *Cynghanedd Groes*:

dal i weld ei dwylo hi

dal ('still')
i weld ('seeing')
ei dwylo hi ('her hands')

'still seeing her hands'

dal i weld | ei dwylo hi
d l / | d l (h)/

or:

a hen gam yn ei gymell   (Gerallt Lloyd Owen 'Cilmeri' 20ᵗʰ C)

a ('and')
hen ('an old')
gam ('wrong')
yn ei gymell ('driving him')

'driven by an old wrong'[1]

a hen gam | yn ei gymell
(h) n g /m | n   g /m

(ii) the letter 'n'

'*n*' is considered to be a soft, weak consonant that would barely register on the X-ray of the word, and as such may be disregarded if it is the first letter in the bar. (When it appears as the first letter of the first bar it is called *n wreiddgoll*, when it appears as the first letter of the second bar it is called *n ganolgoll*).

(a) **un rhan fach o'r hyn a fu**   (Emyr Lewis '*Enwogrwydd*' 20ᵗʰ C)

un ('one')
rhan ('part')
fach ('small')
o'r hyn ('of that')
a fu ('which was')

'one small part of that which was'

un rhan fach | o'r hyn a fu
n rh n f/   r h n   f/

if we disregard the first *n* we recognise this line as an example of *Cynghanedd Groes*.

(b) **Y mae ias yn ei miwsig**   (Emyr Lewis '*Morfudd Llwyn Owen*' 20ᵗʰ C)

[1] All the English renderings from 'Cilmeri' are taken from Dafydd Johnston's translation.

y mae ('there is')
ias ('a thrill')
yn ('in')
ei ('her')
miwsig ('music')

Y mae ias | yn ei miwsig
m   / s   n   m / s

the definition of this type of line is debatable; some would argue
that it is an example of *Cynghanedd Draws* with a bridge over the
middle '*n*', others that it is example of *Cynghanedd Groes* with an
n ganolgoll.

(c) **Ni fydd yn gyrru'i fyddin**   (Twm Morys '*Drysau*' 21st C)

Ni fydd ('he will not')
yn gyrru ('be sending')
'i fyddin ('his army')

Ni fydd | yn gyrru'i fyddin
n f /dd | (n g r)   f / dd

Disregarding the first '*n*', this line can be recognised as an example
of *Cynghanedd Draws.*

(iii) the repeated consonant

When the same consonant is repeated before the stress on either
side of the bar line – with no other consonants between the pair – it
need only be balanced by one matching consonant, e.g.

Gwag yw alaw heb galon   (Tudur Dylan Jones '*Mur*' 21st C)

gwag ('empty')
yw alaw ('is a melody')
heb ('without')
galon ('a heart')

'a melody without a heart is an empty melody'

Gwag yw alaw | heb galon
g   g   / l   (b)g / l

where the two '*g*'s in the first part of the line are matched by only
one '*g*' in the second, forming a *Cynghanedd Draws.*

(iv) synalœpha – *ceseilio*

Because *cynghanedd* is ruled by the ear and not by the eye, a line
which might seem on paper to be more than seven syllables long,
might well shrink when spoken. The merging of one syllable into
another is a characteristic of speech, particularly when the first of
the adjoining syllables ends with a vowel and the second begins
with a vowel. Listen to this line:

mascara a reda dros rudd   (Meirion W. Jones 'Judy
                                    Garland' 20ᵗʰ C)

mascara ('mascara')
a reda ('that runs')
dros ('down')
rudd ('cheek')

'mascara runs down your cheek'

This *Cynghanedd Sain* can be counted either as eight syllables –
where the '*a*' at the end of '*mascara*' and the '*a*' which is the next
word '***a***' are both given due utterance, or as seven syllables, where
these two '*a*'s merge into one: *mascarareda*.

The technical term for this process is 'synalœpha' (or 'elision'),
in Welsh *ceseilio*.

(v) special consonants

'c' in the word 'ac' softens to a 'g' sound:

ac ail-fyw ei glwyfau o   (Gerallt Lloyd Owen 'Cilmeri' 20ᵗʰ C)

ac ('and')
ail-fyw ('re-live')
ei ('his')
glwyfau o ('wounds')

'and I relive his wounds'[2]

This line may seem unbalanced to the eye, yet to the ear it is in
perfect harmony, since the '*c*' in the first word '*ac*' will soften to
'*g*' as it forms part of the '*ac*'.

[2] *Ibid.*

Ac ail fyw | ei glwyfau o
   g   l f/ | gl   f /

't' softens to 'd' after 's':

Un nos da cyn distewi   (Gwion Lynch *'Mam'* 20th C)

un ('one')
nos ('night')
da ('good')
cyn ('before')
distewi ('to become silent')

'one good night before becoming silent'

While this line might seem out of harmony, as the '*t*' in the second
bar doesn't look as if it should chime with the '*d*' of the first bar:

Un nos da | cyn distewi
  n   s d/ | c n d st/

once read aloud, one hears immediately that the '*t*' in fact makes a
'*d*' sound. This is because it follows the consonant '*s*' and this is
true of English pronunciation too (try saying the word 'stand' out
loud and consider how the '*t*' softens to '*d*'). And so we see that the
line is indeed balanced and creates an example of *Cynghanedd
Draws*. (Remember that the first '*n*' sound of any line need not find
a corresponding consonant to balance with it in the second bar.)

Un nos da | cyn distewi
   s d/ | sd/

consonants that 'swallow' one another

In other cases, a strong consonant may 'swallow' a softer consonant
that immediately follows or precedes it.

    '*c*' swallows '*g*' to give a '*c*' sound. The same sort of ruling
applies to '*ff*' and '*f*'; where these two sounds follow each other the
prevailing sound is '*ff*', and so there is no need to 'balance' both
sets of consonants. And the same goes for '*l*' and '*ll*' as in the
following example:

Mae ôl llafn fy mwyell i   (Gerallt Lloyd Owen 'Cilmeri' 20th C)

Mae ôl ('the mark')
llafn ('of the blade')
fy mwyell i ('of my axe')

'My axe's blade has left its mark'

Mae ôl llafn | fy mwyell i
m   (l)ll / | f m   ll /

The same principle applies to the letters '*p*' and '*b*' (where '*p*' is the prevailing sound) and '*d*' and '*t*', (where '*t*' prevails).

The following line is an interesting example in that it shows two curious balancing acts:

Nid tyweirch ond dyhead   (Dic Jones '*Clawdd Offa*' 21st C)

Nid ('not')
tyweirch ('clumps of earth')
ond ('but')
dyhead ('a longing')

Nid tyweirch | ond dyhead
n d t /   nd d   /

At first sight this line seems completely unbalanced. But when we realise that '*d*' is swallowed by '*t*' if these two consonants follow each other immediately, then we see that in the first bar the pattern is '*n t*'. In the second, when we listen carefully, we hear that two '*d*'s next to each other harden to create the sound '*t*'. And so we see that the consonantal pattern is in fact:

Nid tyweirch | ond dyhead
n   t / | n   t   /

The principle that claims that the two '*d*'s next to each other create a '*t*' sound is quite contentious, and so is the claim that '*d*' + '*h*' = '*t*' or '*g*' + '*g*' = '*c*'. In a recent *cynghanedd* Festival held in Tŷ Newydd, these kinds of examples were the subject of hot debate. The overriding rule is that one must be true to one's ear!

Here are some further examples:

Cannoedd o gesig gwynion (T. Arfon Williams '*Ewyn*' 20th C)

Cannoedd ('hundreds')
o ('of')
gesig ('horses')
gwynion ('white')

'hundreds of white horses'

Cannoedd I o gesig gwynion
c / n   I g s g g / n

At first, it seems an unbalanced line, but if we accept that two '*g*' sounds next to each other harden to create a '*c*' sound then the pattern is different:

Cannoedd I o gesig gwynion
c / n   I g s c / n

Ni allwn fod hebot ti   (Mei Mac '*I Nia*' 20th C)

Ni allwn ('I could not')
fod ('be')
hebot ti ('without you')

Ni allwn fod I hebot I ti
**   od I   ot**
**   h /   I t/**

With no apparent rhyme or balance of consonants the eye cannot detect a trace of *cynghanedd* here. But the ear will tell us that the '*d*' at the end of the first bar '*fod*', placed next to the '*h*' at the beginning of the second bar '*hebot*' will harden to create a '*t*' sound. Thus the rhyme is in fact '*ot*' – which corresponds to the '*ot*' at the end of '*hebot*'. The same rule applies to the balance of consonants needed to complete the harmony in a *Cynghanedd Sain* between the beginning of the second and third bars. The '*t*' sound prevails, over the bar line to match the '*t*' at the beginning of the word '*ti*'!
And so the aural pattern is:

Ni allwn fod I hebot I ti
**   ot   ot**
**   t/   t/**

which is perfect!

4.2 More Fun and Games!

(i) *Y Groes o Gyswllt*

This is a special type of *Cynghanedd Groes* where, in order to
balance the consonants between the two bars of the line, it is
necessary to borrow the last consonant of the first bar. The
composition of a *Cynghanedd Groes* o *Gyswllt* demands a high
level of skill, but though it seems complicated, it does in fact
increase the possibilities and open the door to many more beautiful
lines:

> **Cnawd yn y co' nid yw'n cau**   (Gerallt Lloyd Owen
> 'Cilmeri' 20th C)
>
> *Cnawd* ('flesh')
> *yn yn co* ('in the memory')
> *nid yw'n cau* ('does not close')
>
> 'in the memory the flesh still gapes'[3]

Upon examination it seems that the first consonant in the first bar,
'*c*', is not matched in the second bar.

> **Cnawd yn y co | nid yw'n cau**
> **cn   d   n   c/|n d   n c/**

However, if we step backwards over the line, from the second bar
into the first, we see that the last consonant there is in fact the same
as the first i.e. '*c*'. We can now borrow this '*c*' to form a perfect
harmony:

> cndn**c**/
> **c**ndnc/

And indeed, we can step backwards over more than one consonant
if needs be.

   The next example is complex indeed. Not only does it borrow a
consonant across the bar line, but it also depends on the fact that the
consonant '*t*' softens to a '*d*' sound when it follows the consonant '*ll*'.

---

[3] *Ibid.*

Dwi'm yn dallt y mynd a dod   (Mei Mac '*Paham*' 20th C)

Dwi'm yn dallt ('I don't understand')
y ('the')
mynd ('coming')
a ('and')
dod ('going')

'I don't understand the coming and going'

Dwi'm yn dallt I y mynd a dod
d   m n d/ llt I   m nd   d /

or, if we obey the ear we have the pattern:

d m n d / d I m n d /

which gives a balance – over the bar line – and therefore makes a
perfect example of *Cynghanedd Groes o Gyswllt*.

(ii) Rhymes on the barline

Sometimes the last word in the bar needs to borrow a consonant
from the beginning of the next bar in order to complete the rhyme.

Fel eco drwy waelod arch   (Alan Llwyd '*Yn Eisteddfod Cwm
Rhymni*' 20th C)

In this example we see how '*eco*' borrows the '*d*' at the beginning
of the word '*drwy*' in order to tease the ear into hearing '*ec<u>od</u>*'
which in turn rhymes with '*wael<u>od</u>*'.

Fel ('like')
eco ('an echo')
drwy ('through')
waelod ('the bottom')
arch ('of a coffin')

Fel eco I drwy waelod I arch
**   o I d   od I**
**   w /   I a /**

Note that in this example of Cynghanedd Sain, the match between
the second and third bars depends on a vowel alone. When two words
in these positions begin with a vowel, then they automatically form
a balance since any two are considered to match one another,
whereas the match between consonants has to be identical.

4.3 and finally . . .

. . . what about lines that are multi-*cynghanedd*, i.e. lines that are
simultaenously more than one type of *cynghanedd*?

Hen yw'n Hanwen yn ei henaint

Hen ('old')
yw'n ('is our')
Hanwen ('Anwen')
yn ('in')
ei ('her')
henaint ('old age')

'Our Anwen is such an old, old woman'

As an example of *Cynghanedd Groes o Gyswllt* (where we reach
back over the bar line to 'borrow' some consonants in order to have
a perfect balance) we can divide the line as follows:

Hen yw'n Hanwen | yn ei henaint
h n   n h/n   n   h/n

As an example of *Cynghanedd Sain* we can divide the line in three
like this:

Hen | yw'n Hanwen | yn ei henaint
en   en
**   h/n   h/n**

And as an example of *Cynghanedd Lusg* we divide it in two and note the internal rhyme between the first and second bars:

Hen yw'n Hanwen | yn ei henaint
           en   **en**

CHAPTER 5

Music in Twenty-Four Measures

The verbs we use in Welsh to describe the process of creating a poem in *cynghanedd* are interesting and reveal something about the psyche behind the art. I have already mentioned that the pieces themselves are called *cerddi*, which is closely associated with the modern Welsh word for music, *cerddoriaeth*. One does not, or at least very rarely, 'write' a line of *cynghanedd* as such. It is almost always a case of 'working' (*gweithio*) or 'composing' (*cyfansoddi*) a line.

Some, however, claim that lines of *cynghanedd* are neither 'worked' nor 'composed', but rather they are 'found', suggesting that the poet is almost a medium that waits to 'happen upon' the lines. I'm not sure if I agree with this entirely, though I understand the sense behind the statement. It is certainly an amazing characteristic of the Welsh language that in everyday speech the tuned ear can find examples of accidental *cynghanedd*. In South Wales, for example, it would be quite ordinary to ask someone: *'Ti ishe dished o dê?'* ('Would you like a cup of tea?'). If we examine this question we can recognise it as a line of *Cynghanedd Sain*:

```
ti ishe | dished | o dê
   e | d    ed |
      | d  /    |   d/
```

Other frequently-used sayings have been lifted from poems written in *cynghanedd*, where the original context has long been forgotten. For example, on noticing signs of old age – a wrinkle or a grey hair – one might sigh: *henaint ni ddaw ei hunan* ('old age doesn't come alone'). This line has by now reached idiomatic or even proverbial status in the Welsh language, but it was probably first composed by Rhys Evans (1779–1867) who uses it as the third line of an *englyn*. It is used again, within quotation marks, as a first line in a famous *englyn* by John Morris Jones (1864–1929), and Ellis Owen (1789–1868) also uses it as a first line to one of his *englynion*, where again it appears in quotation marks.

But this begs the question – what exactly is an *englyn*? In poetry a line of *cynghanedd* rarely exists on its own. Lines of *cynghanedd* are put together in different 'measures'. In *cerdd dafod* there are twenty-four such measures.[1] When, for example, the competition requirements of the eisteddfod state that the composition for the Chair must be written in the 'traditional measures', it is to these twenty-four measures that it refers. An *englyn* is one such measure.

During the last century, poets largely confined themselves to about four of these measures, but the past few years have seen an effort to revive some of the less fashionable ones, and indeed to create new ones. There is an increasing realisation that opportunities are being missed by not using the full range of measures available. The Chair at the St David's National Eisteddfod held in 2002 went to Myrddin ap Dafydd for a composition that was far more ambitious in its range of measures than had been seen for decades.

John Morris Jones, author of the most thorough compilation of the rules of *cerdd dafod*, begins his chapter on the twenty-four measures by explaining that they derive from lines of four or six beats. This notion of 'beats' is an interesting one. He explains that counting the 'beat' of a line was much more important than counting syllables. To this day, as seen in the previous chapters, while the number of syllables has to be observed, equally the stress and beat of the line remain important.

The measures can be sorted into three main categories – *Englyn*, *Cywydd* and *Awdl*. (This is somewhat confusing, as the term *awdl* is also used to describe a poem written in more than one of the twenty-four measures and is the usual requirement in the Chair competition in the eisteddfod). I shall not attempt to translate the names of each measure, as this would be meaningless since the terms are, to all intents and purposes, proper nouns.

In the next section I have relied heavily on the template laid out by Roy Stephens in his useful work *Yr Odliadur*.[2] I have decided not to outline the patterns of all the twenty-four measures as many

---

[1] See chapter 2.
[2] *Yr Odliadur*, Roy Stephens, Llandysul (1978) – an indispensable rhyming dictionary for any student of *cynghanedd*.

are virtually obsolete in contemporary practice. My selection is largely whimsical though it does include the most popular types.

In the examples given, the letters a, b, c, d etc. will denote rhymes, where 'a' rhymes with 'a', 'b' with 'b' etc. Evidently, each line must contain *cynghanedd*, but the capital letter 'G' however will denote the need to form *cynghanedd* across two lines i.e. between the end of one line and the middle of the next.

1 *Englynion*

There are eight different types of *englyn*, most have four lines, but not all.

Englyn Unodl Union

.... a – ...G	(10 syllables, divided 7+3, 8+2 or 9+1)
.........G ... a	(6 syllables)
.... a	(7 syllables)
....a	(7 syllables)

This is one of the most popular measures today – so popular that on the whole, when people refer simply to an *englyn*, they mean the *englyn unodl union* to give its full title. Its brevity – 30 syllables in total – makes it memorable. It demands pithy expression and concise thinking (some say that the haiku is similar to it). Its tone and register however can vary greatly, and an *englyn* can be used effectively to convey the epigrammatic, lyrical, didactic or satirical. It can also be humorous – though a comic *englyn* is regarded by many as the most difficult of all to pull off. An *englyn* can stand alone or form part of a sequence. If one of the words in the last line of an *englyn* is repeated in the first line of the next, such a sequence is called *cadwyn* ('chain'); if, as well as this, each *englyn* has the same rhyme, then the sequence is called *gosteg* (this term cannot be translated).

An important feature of this measure is that the second line MUST end in an unstressed syllable, and in the final pair of lines one ends with a stressed syllable and the other with an unstressed syllable (see *cywydd* below). The first pair of lines is known as *paladr* and the second as *esgyll*. The quality of an *englyn unodl union* can often be measured by the strength of its last line.

Indeed, expert *englynion* composers often agree that the way to a fine *englyn* is to work backwards – this, they claim, ensures that the whole *englyn* leads to the last line and thus to a climax.

> *Dydd byr yw pob diwedd byd; anadliad*
> *Yw cenhedlaeth hefyd;*
> *Nid yw Hanes ond ennyd;*
> *A fu ddoe a fydd o hyd.*

> (Gerallt Lloyd Owen 'Cilmeri' 20ᵗʰ C)

> Every world's end is a short day;
> a generation is no more than a breath;
> History is but a moment;
> what was yesterday will be forever.

Have you recognised the first line as an example of *Cynghanedd Draws*, and the last pair as examples of *Cynghanedd Groes*?

As a matter of interest, there is also such a thing as an upside-down *englyn unodl union*, though it is much more rare than its right-way-up counterpart. Known as the *englyn crwca*, its pattern is as follows:

.... a	(7 syllables)
.... a	(7 syllables)
...............a – ....a...G	(10 syllables: 7+3, 8+2, 9+1)
.... G.........a	(6 syllables)

The next two types of *englyn* listed below have only three lines:

Englyn penfyr

This rather uncommon measure follows the pattern:

.... a – ...G	(10 syllables: 7+3, 8+2 or 9+1)
...........G...........a	(6 syllables)
.......................a	(7 syllables)

Y wlad mewn gwisg o flodau – yn galw
Dwy galon i lwybrau
Yr ifanc drwy yr hafau.

(Dosbarth Tanygroes '*Y Flwyddyn*' 20th C)[3]

The countryside, in its floral dress, calls
two hearts to roam the paths
of the young through summer days.

The first line of the *englyn penfyr* (like the *englyn unodl union*) is in fact a line and a half, where the first part comes to an end after the main rhyme 'a'. The second part of the first line (the section after the main rhyme 'a') must form *cynghanedd* with the first part of the second line. The technical term for the caesura after the main rhyme in the first line is called *gwant* and is characteristically denoted by a small dash or hyphen.

In the above example, the first seven syllables in the first line form *Cynghanedd Draws*, and the third line is also an example of *Cynghanedd Draws*.

Englyn Milwr

This is a popular measure as it somehow creates a sparse atmosphere. It is one of the most terse and concise of all the measures. (It is also one of the measures that was thrown out of the classic *cerdd dafod* code but has withstood the test of time and survived probably because of the qualities mentioned above). In the *englyn milwr* each line is a self-contained *cynghanedd*.

..................a	(7 syllables)
..................a	(7 syllables)
..................a	(7 syllables)

Er bod bysedd y beddau
Yn deilwriaid doluriau
Cnawd yn y co' nid yw'n cau.

(Gerallt Lloyd Owen 'Cilmeri' 20th C)

---

[3] *Barddas,* Gorffennaf 1992, pp. 28–30.

Although the grave's fingers
are skilled tailors of wounds
in the memory the flesh still gapes.[4]

In this example, the first line is a *Cynghanedd Lusg*, the second a
Cynghanedd Groes (where the first '*n*' is ignored) and the third line
a *Cynghanedd Groes o Gyswllt* (where the second half of the line
'borrows' the consonant '*c*' from the first half).

Englyn Cyrch

The word *cyrch* is the technical term for an internal rhyme. In the
englyn cyrch, the last pair of lines has an internal rhyme between
the end of the third line and middle of the fourth line. Lines one,
two and four rhyme together.

.... a	(7 syllables)
.... a	(7 syllables)
.... b	(7 syllables)
...........b............ a	(7 syllables)

> *Daw yr eirlys drwy'r hirlwm*
> *A'u sidan can yn y cwm*
> *A bydd cawod o flodau*
> *Yn bywhau y lloriau llwm.*

> (Dosbarth Tanygroes '*Y Flwyddyn*' 20th C)

Snowdrops will emerge through the winter months
their white silk covering the valley
and a shower of flowers
will bring life to the barren land.

---

[4] The translations of all the verses taken from 'Cilmeri' by Gerallt
Lloyd Owen in this section are by Dafydd Johnston. See *Modern Poetry in
Translation*, No 7, London (1995), pp. 126–144; ed Daniel Weissbort.

Englyn Proest Cyfnewidiog

This type of englyn follows the pattern:

.... p	(7 syllables)
.... p	(7 syllables)
.... p	(7 syllables)
.... p	(7 syllables)

where p stands for *proest* or half-rhyme. This is a rhyme where the end consonant is the same and the vowel is different but of a similar length.

E.g. *tân* ('fire') makes a *proest* or half-rhyme with *Môn* ('Anglesey'), where '*â*' and '*ô*' are different vowels but equal in length, and the final consonant '*n*' is the same in both words.

Similarly, *cap* ('cap') makes a *proest* or half-rhyme with *twp* ('stupid'), where '*a*' and '*w*' are different vowels but equal in length and the final consonant '*p*' is the same in both words.

A variation on this is the **Englyn Proest Cadwynog** where the pattern is slightly more complicated, as lines one and three and two and four are full rhymes but where the two pairs of full rhymes form a half rhyme or *proest* with one another.

.... a	(7 syllables)
.... b	(7 syllables)
.... a	(7 syllables)
.... b	(7 syllables)

('a' rhymes with 'a' and 'b' with 'b', but 'a' and 'b' also form a half-rhyme).

To make matters slightly more complicated, in measures that aren't specifically dedicated to the half-rhyme, then to use the half-rhyme within a line is not permitted and disqualifies the validity of the *cynghanedd* in that stanza!

2 *Cywyddau*

There are four different types of '*cywydd*', of which I shall describe
three (the fourth being the rare **cywydd llosgyrnog**).

Awdl-Gywydd

.... b   (7 syllables)
.... b.............. a   (7 syllables)

where 'a' is the main rhyme of the stanza as a whole.

> *Pan gaf innau'r lliwiau'n llwyr*
> *ar hyd yr hwyr ar dy draeth,*
> *caf innau eiriau drwy'r nos*
> *sy'n aros yn eu hiraeth.*

> When I finally find
> the evening colours on your sands,
> I find too the language of longing.
> It stays with me through the night.

(Tudur Dylan Jones '*Llais*' 21st C)

Cywydd Deuair Hirion

Along with the *englyn unodl union*, this is by far the most popular
of all the measures. And just as the *englyn unodl union* is usually
called simply *englyn*, the *cywydd deuair hirion* is usually referred
to simply as *cywydd*. It is a flexible measure that can stand as a
single couplet or it can run to dozens of lines. As such it is ideal for
narrative and descriptive passages.

.... a   (7 syllables)
.... a   (7 syllables)

> *Yn neufyd un ystafell*
> *Mae'r byw a'r marw mor bell.*

(Gerallt Lloyd Owen 'Cilmeri' 20th C)

In the twin worlds of a single room
the living and the dead are so far apart.

An important feature of this measure is that each pair of lines must have one ending on the stressed syllable and the other on the unstressed syllable:

ystafell

bell

This variation in stress pattern at the end of every line, as well as the unpredictable nature of *cynghanedd* (see chapter 3) makes the *cywydd* a particularly melodic form.

Cywydd Deuair Fyrion

This is a condensed version of the *cywydd deuair hirion* (perhaps it would help to learn that *hirion* means 'long' and *fyrion* means 'short'!)

.... a   (4 syllables)
.... a   (4 syllables)

> *fan hyn gefn nos*
> *nawr mae'n aros*
> *un wefr gyfrin*
> *yn groyw ar sgrîn.*

> (Llion Jones '*E-Pistol@*'21st C)

Just here, in the deep night,
there remains
one secret thrill
crystal clear on a screen.

Here again the alternating pattern of stressed and unstressed line-endings must be observed.

3 *Awdlau*

There are twelve different types in this category and most of these
measures offer the opportunity to create *cynghanedd* over many
more beats as the long lines are divided by rhymes after relatively
short sections.

Take for example the **Rhupunt Byr** that follows the pattern:

............b............b............a   (4 syllables, 4 syllables,
                                                4 syllables)

where 'a' is the main rhyme in the stanza.

> *Mae'r haul mor hen | yn wawr o wên | ar dir y rhos.*
>
> (Tudur Dylan Jones '*Y Daith*' 21st C)

The ancient sun dawns a smile on the moor.

A characteristic of this measure is its complex rhyming rule. If 'b'
does not end with a stressed syllable, then it must form what in
Welsh we would describe as a 'double rhyme' i.e. where both the
last syllables rhyme. Perhaps you will recall the notes on rhyme at
the beginning of chapter 3: while *dysgu* ('to learn') rhymes with *du*
('black'), it would need a word such as *cysgu* ('to sleep') to form a
double rhyme.

However, if 'b' ends in a stressed syllable, then the first two
sections of the line must form two separate *cynganeddion* and the
second and third section must together form a line of *cynghanedd
groes*!

Rhupunt Hir is a variation on the **Rhupunt Byr** and follows
the pattern:

.... b .... b   (4 syllable, 4 syllable)
.... b .... a   (4 syllable, 4 syllable)

> *Y gân i gyd yn hardd o hyd*
> *a daw i'r byd y wawr o bell.*
>
> (Tudur Dylan Jones '*Y Daith*' 21st C)

The whole song is forever beautiful
and from afar the day dawns on the world.

And now an example taken from the winning entry in the Chair competition of the 2004 National Eisteddfod. Here we see the *rhupunt hir* where 'b' forms part of an unstressed syllable:

Hunwch, blantos, heno'n ddiddos,
Dall yw dunos i dwyll dynion.

(Huw Meirion Edwards *'Cwsg y Dedwydd'*, 21st C)

Sleep little children, sleep soundly tonight,
the darkness is blind to the deceit of men.

Cyhydedd Fer

This is simply a number of eight-syllable lines sharing a common end rhyme. The last word of the line can be stressed or unstressed (see *cywydd deuair hirion* above). Although this is a flexible measure just like the *cywydd deuair hirion*, poets since the days of Dafydd ap Gwilym have shown preference for the seven-syllable lines.

…………………….. a   (8 syllables)
…………………….. a   (8 syllables)

Ai dod yr wyt i gadw'r oed
I liwio cân rhwng dail y coed?

(Tudur Dylan Jones *'Arianrhod Rhwng y Coed'* 21st C)

Are you coming to keep a promise
to colour a song between the leaves?

Cyhydedd Naw Ban

Given that *naw* is the Welsh for 'nine', the reader will not be surprised to learn that this measure is composed of nine-syllable lines. This measure usually comes in a group of four lines bound together with a common end rhyme.

.... a   (9 syllables)
.... a   (9 syllables)
.... a   (9 syllables)
.... a   (9 syllables)

An example of this is taken from the *awdl* that won the Chair in the National Eisteddfod in 1950 for Gwilym R. Tilsey for a poem in praise of the miner:

> *Newid a ddaeth ar y dydd weithion*
> *I ŵr diwyd y llethrau duon;*
> *Daeth i'r lofa dalog swyddogion,*
> *A mud weithwyr lle bu cymdeithion.*

(Gwilym R. Tilsley *'Y Glöwr'* 20ᵗʰ C)

> Things changed
> for the hard-working man of the black coal-face.
> Self-important officials came to the mine,
> and silent workers where there were comrades once.

The *cynghanedd* in each line follows the same principles as *cynghanedd* in the more common seven-syllable lines with two main beats (and thus two main 'bars') in the *draws*, *groes* and *lusg*, and three in *sain*. The consonantal match takes its cue from where the stress lies in each 'bar'.

Thus the first line of the above example is made of *cynghanedd draws*:

Newid a ddaeth | ar y dydd weithion
d   dd / th   (r) d dd   / th

Cyhydedd Hir

.... b .... b   (5 syllables, 5 syllables)
.... b .... a   (5 syllables, 4 syllables)

Here, there are two separate instances of *cynghanedd* in the first line, both bound together with a common rhyme, while in the second line the two phrases form one *cynghanedd* but with two rhymes binding it, on the one hand to the preceding lines and, on the other, to the main rhyme of the stanza. Note how in the following example the poet has started a new line after the first five syllables thus varying the pattern slightly to:

```
.............. b                        (5 syllables)
.............. b                        (5 syllables)
.............. b ............ a         (5 syllables, 4 syllables)
```

> *Gyfaill, mi'th gofiaf,*
> *Dy ben heulwen haf*
> *A glyn y gaeaf galon gywir.*
> *Ym mhob dyn mab dau*
> *Gwelit y golau*
> *Ac yng nghraidd y gau angerdd y gwir.*

(Waldo Williams '*Gyfaill, mi'th gofiaf*' 20th C)

> I remember you, friend –
> Your summer sunshine head
> And vale of the winter
> True heart.
> In each man, son of two,
> You would see light –
> At falsehood's core
> The force of true.[5]

(translated by Tony Conran)

Hir a Thoddaid

After the *englyn* (*unodl union*), *cywydd* (*deuair hirion*), the *hir a thoddaid* has been the most common measure in the recent period. The long ten-syllable lines make it a leisurely measure. If the tempo for a *cywydd* lies between *andante* and *allegretto*, then the *hir a thoddaid* is between *andante* and *lento*.

---

[5] *The Peacemakers*, Waldo Williams, translated by Tony Conran, Gomer, (1997), p. 146.

The pattern is:

```
............................................. a (10 syllables)
............................................. a (10 syllables)
+
...........................a............... b (7+ 3, 8+ 2, 9+1 syllables)
...............b............................ a (10 syllables)
```

But it is quite common to see four or six lines preceding the final pair as in the following example taken from the work of the brilliant Dic Jones. (I have heard Dic Jones, a farmer, mention anecdotally that he would compose lines for *hir a thoddaid* to the beat of the metronome in the milking-parlour.)

> *Mae fy ngobeithion yn rhan ohonot,*
> *Mae fy nioddef a'm hofnau'n eiddot,*
> *Yn d'oriau euraid, fy malchder erot,*
> *Yn d'oriau isel, fy ngweddi drosot,*
> *Mae'n well byd y man lle bôt, – mae deunydd*
> *Fy holl lawenydd, fy nghyfaill, ynot.*

(Dic Jones 'Cyfaill' 20th C)

> My hopes are a part of you,
> my suffering and fears are yours,
> in your golden hours you are my pride,
> in your dark hours, you are my prayer;
> wherever you may be the world is a better place –
> you, my friend, are the making of my every joy.

More Patterns

The remaining seven measures of *cerdd dafod* missing from the above exposition are:

(i) Tawddgyrch Cadwynog

```
..................b ............... c     (8 syllables, 4+4)
..................c............... a     (8 syllables, 4+4)
..................b............... c     (8 syllables, 4+4)
..................c............... a     (8 syllables, 4+4)
```

```
.................d.....…..........  d      (8 syllables, 4+4)
.................d.............  a         (8 syllables, 4+4)
.................d.....……......  d        (8 syllables, 4+4)
.................d..............  a         (8 syllables, 4+4)
```

(ii) **Byr a thoddaid**

```
...................... a – …..             (10 syllables: 7+3, 8+2, 9+1)
............. a                             (6 syllables)
................... a                       (8 syllables)
................... a                       (8 syllables)
...................... a – …..             (10 syllables: 7+3, 8+2, 9+1)
............. a                             (6 syllables)
```

(iii) **Toddaid**

```
......................... a – …b           (10 syllables: 7 +3, 8+2, 9+1)
...........b...........  a                 (9 syllables)
```

(iv) **Gwawdodyn**

```
...................... a                    (9 syllables)
...................... a                    (9 syllables)
...................... a – …b              (10 syllables: 7 +3, 8+2, 9+1)
...........b...........  a                 (9 syllables)
```

(v) **Gwawdodyn Hir**

```
...................... a                    (9 syllables)
...................... a                    (9 syllables)
...................... a                    (9 syllables)
...................... a                    (9 syllables)
......................a – …b               (10 syllables: 7 +3, 8+2, 9+1)
...........b...........  a                 (9 syllables)
```

(vi) **Clogyrnach**

………………….. a	(8 syllables)
………………….. a	(8 syllables)
…………….b……………b	(5 syllables + 5 syllables)
……b……a	(6 syllables)

(vii) **Cyrch a chwta**

………………….. a	(8 syllables)
………………….. a	(8 syllables)
…………….b……………b	(5 + 5 syllables)
……b……a	(6 syllables)

*   *   *

But *cynghanedd* is a living art form and experimentation in the range of measures is becoming increasingly apparent in the work of poets today. The use of *cynghanedd* in *vers libre* can also be found where end rhymes and syllable counts are largely ignored but the basics of 'harmonization' are observed.

CHAPTER 6

'What's englyn *when it's English?'*

'<u>*Da*</u>' is 'fine'; '*pysgod*' is 'fish' – '*isho bwyd*'
   is '<u>Boy! Am I peckish!</u>'
 '*Dwyn*' is 'steal', '*desgil*' is 'dish';
 What's '*englyn*' when it's English?

In this *englyn*, whose first three lines were composed by Twm
Morys and last line by Myrddin ap Dafydd, light-hearted though it
might seem, the final, unanswered question is significant. It
reminds us that *englyn* is one of those words that cannot be
translated from Welsh into English. And the simple answer to the
question 'What's *englyn* when it's English' is probably: 'Nothing
much'. After all, one will need more than words to translate a
tradition that is at least fifteen hundred years old. Without the
tradition, there is no real meaning.

It is difficult enough to explain what an *englyn* is to the
uninitiated amongst the Welsh-speaking audience. This is an
extract from a poem by Ifor ap Glyn which sets about showing how
difficult a task this is. The translation is by Nigel Jenkins.

Englyns
[. . .]
Englyns are not a kind of *bratwurst* . . .
a *bratwurst* has no trouble raising laughs . . .
especially if it's a 'stand-up' *bratwurst*.

Englyns can't be compared to dogs.
An *englyn* will neither give rise to fleas,
nor fetch your new slippers as you take your ease,
it'll simply inform you that the old pair
were so much better than these.

Englyns are also unlike ashtrays;
they can hold things that shine

77

as well as what's ashen,
and no parlour should be without one
in case a poet should call.

Because *englyns* are ancient –
a kind of bardic bouncing cheque –
they're like last night's curry, inclined to 'repeat'
and after fifteen hundred years –
they're still pretty neat.

Writing the little devils
is as much as ever a fag,
but things will be somewhat different
when we've *englyns* that 'boil in the bag'.

We don't yet have '*englyns*'[1] that 'boil in the bag', but a few rare poets have attempted to write an *englyn* in English. Take these examples by two experts in the craft of *cerdd dafod*.

The Night

No hymn of birds, no tremor – save the sounds
     Of the sea's sad tenor,
   The stars ascend in splendour,
   And the dark creeps round the door.

                              Dic Jones

On every grave I hear a groan – a sigh
     As old as creation,
   Unmeasured in emotion,
   Could it be, maybe, my own?

                       Gerallt Lloyd Owen

---

[1] It should be noted that the plural of *englyn* is *englynion* not '*englyns*' (as used by Ifor ap Glyn – where the 's' is added for comic effect as it is taken from the English way of forming plurals).

It can just about be done. But both Dic Jones and Gerallt Lloyd Owen are outstanding poets and outstanding practitioners of *cynghanedd*. They are very much the exception that proves the rule. Because, quite apart from the absence of a comparable tradition in English, there are two other reasons why an *englyn*, or indeed any measure written in *cynghanedd*, doesn't have the same resonance, and isn't thus as effective in English as in Welsh. As we have already seen, Welsh is a heavily stressed language, English is not. Furthermore, we have learnt that the first consonant of every word can mutate into another consonant in Welsh – two inherent characteristics of the language that make the possibility of composing *cynghanedd* in Welsh a very different proposition from trying to do so in English.

These are some of the same reasons why translating poems written in *cynghanedd* is so difficult. At best, translating poetry is a frustrating task. The particular fusion of sound and sense in any poem is unique to the language of that poem, and the translator faces difficult decisions with every word, as often rhyme must give way to reason, meaning to measure, sound to sense or vice versa. In poems written in *cynghanedd*, however, the fusion between these elements is even closer. It can be said that translating a poem written in *cynghanedd* is akin to attempting to translate a song where both the words and the music must change. What's left is at best the palest reflection of the original, and often translations of poems written in *cynghanedd* leave the reader with the false impression that the original is banal and base, while in reality the original poem is beautiful and sublime.

Successful examples of translations of *cynghanedd*, as indeed original poems in the craft in English are rare.[2] One such rare example is the following *cywydd*, which, as I understand, Twm Morys wrote for the purpose of illustrating *cynghanedd* to an English-speaking audience.

---

[2] I have seen examples of verses in books and on websites that purport to be in *cynghanedd*, but which almost invariably are not. See chapter 7.

My First Love Was A Plover

My first love was a plover.
Beautiful things her wings were.
Tiny eyes shining at night
(though mainly in the moonlight).
We ate cakes by a lakeside,
I caressed her crest and cried
all night. Then the kite called,
unshaven and dishevelled.
He saw from the bristling sedge
my playmate's handsome plumage.
She made a tryst, kissed the kite
so dearly in the starlight.
I thought of only one thing:
my plover lover leaving.

Twm Morys (*'Ofn fy Het'*, Cyhoeddiadau Barddas, p. 44)

There have been other poets who, unlike Twm Morys, do not have the advantage of speaking Welsh fluently but who have set about learning the rules of *cynghanedd* quite consciously and have used the craft to enrich their writing in English.[3]

There is evidence that William Barnes, after visiting Wales in 1831, set about learning the rules of *cynghanedd* and perhaps the most famous example of his attempt to write *cynghanedd* in English is the line:

Do lean down low in Linden Lea

which approximates to the *Cynghanedd Groes*, but fails to balance the first 'd' in the first bar with an equivalent 'd' in the second bar.

Do lean down low | in Linden Lea
d l nd   n l / l n l nd n l /

Alan Llwyd, twice winner of both the Chair and Crown at the National Eisteddfod, has established that Barnes influenced both

---

[3] See *'Cynghanedd* and English Poetry', Alan Llwyd, *Poetry Wales*, Vol. 14, no. 1, Swansea (1978), pp. 23–58.

Thomas Hardy and Gerard Manley Hopkins with his love of *cynghanedd*. Alan Llwyd shows how Hardy's poem 'The Last Signal', written after he attended Barnes's funeral, has traces of *cynghanedd* and reminds the reader of Hardy's introduction to the *Select Poems of Willam Barnes* which refers to Barnes's 'ingenious internal rhymes, his subtle juxtaposition of kindred lippings and vowel sounds . . .'

Time and again Alan Llwyd finds approximations of *cynghanedd* in Hardy's verse; e.g.

A light fall of little feet

A light fall | of little feet
⎪   t f / ⎪   t(l) f /

or:

Lay dying that I held dear

Lay dying | that I held dear
⎪   d/   (th t)   ld d /

Alan Llwyd also notes many examples of *cynghanedd* in the work of Wilfred Owen (e.g. 'The shadow of the morrow weighed on men') and explains how Owen might have been introduced to *cynghanedd* through his Welsh connections.

Robert Graves, in an interview with Leslie Norris in 'The Listener'[4] confirms the seminal role *cynghanedd* had in his verse:

> Wales is very important to me; and if asked what was the most important technical influence on my verse I'd say the Welsh. It started with *cynghanedd*.

He goes on to describe how the first poem he ever published in book form was an *englyn* in English. He had been taught the rules of *cynghanedd* by Archdeacon Edwards, whose bardic name was Gwynedd, and his father, Alfred Perceval Graves, in the appendix

---

[4] *The Listener*, 28 May 1970 – Where the crakeberries grow – Robert Graves gives an account of himself to Leslie Norris.

to *Welsh Poetry Old and New in English Verse*,[5] uses the following *englyn* by Robert Graves by way of illustration:

The Will o' the Wisp

See a gleam in the gloaming – out yonder
    It wand'reth bright flaming;
    Its force – that is a fierce thing!
    It draweth men to drowning.

It falls short of perfect *cynghanedd*, but it does at least prove that Graves was well aware of the ancient craft.

Turning to Dylan Thomas, the most famous of Welsh poets who wrote in English, we find considerable debate as to what extent his work is consciously influenced by *cynghanedd*. He himself denied knowledge of the form, and yet, scattered throughout his poems are examples of *cynghanedd*, most famously the line:

    though I sang in my chains like the sea.

In this line the pattern **th s/** heard in 'though I sang' balances with **th s/** heard in 'the sea' and bridges over the **m ch ns l k** of the middle section.

Be that as it may, there can be no question of Gerard Manley Hopkins's debt to *cynghanedd*.[6] A student at the College of St Beuno, St Asaph, Clwyd, he started to learn Welsh and soon was inspired to learn the intricate rules of *cerdd dafod*. He had already noticed Barnes's attempt to write according to the Welsh tradition but notes:

> However his employment of the Welsh *cynghanedd* or chime I do not look on as quite successful. To tell the truth, I think I could do that better, and it is an artificial thing and not much in his line. (I mean like '*Paladore* and *Polly dear*', which is in my judgement more of a miss than a hit.)[7]

[5] *Welsh Poetry Old and New*, Alfred Perceval Graves, Longmans (1912).
[6] Alexandra Lavizzari has written an interesting article on the use of *cynghanedd* in Manley Hopkins's work, published in the *Neue Zuricher Zeitung,* 29th November 2003.
[7] *Poetry Wales,* Vol. 14, p. 29.

I would agree with Hopkins's judgement, and there can be no doubt that he himself progressed to write far more convincingly in *cynghanedd* than Barnes.

Listen to the following lines taken from Hopkins's 'The Wreck of Deutschland'. You will hear how they are almost in perfect harmony:

Warm-laid grave | of a womb-life grey
w rm | d gr / | (f) w m l f gr /

(where the 'r' in 'warm' is hardly heard and the 'b' in 'womb' is of course not heard at all)

Mark, | the mark | is of man's make
ark   ark
m/   m/

A rhyme between bars one and two and a balance between the consonants immediately preceding the stress in bars two and three give an example of *Cynghanedd Sain*.

The down-dugged | ground-hugged | grey
ugged   ugged
gr/   gr/

Cynghanedd Sain lends 'The Windhover' its special flavour too, with its majestic opening line:

I caught this morning | morning's | minion
ing   ing
m / n | m/n

(Don't be deceived by the 'r' in morning as it is not heard – remember that *cynghanedd* is always for the ear not the eye.)

In 'God's Grandeur' there are further examples to be found:

And wears man's smudge | and shares man's smell
nd   rs m n s m /   nd s r s m n s m/

There is a stray 'sh' at the beginning of the second bar, but since the 'd' at the end of 'and' is so soft, one could argue that the balancing-act between the consonants only starts with the letter 'r'.

And a less pure example, but one that nonetheless shows *cynghanedd* playing its part is in the last line of the same poem:

world broods with warm breast . . .

It soon becomes apparent that the heavy alliteration and so-called 'sprung rhythm' so characteristic of Manley Hopkins derives from his understanding of *cynghanedd* and his knowledege of the Welsh language – an understanding and knowledge that allowed him to compose some verse in Welsh.

But one of the best places of all to see *cynghanedd* in the English language is on the front pages of the tabloid press or in advertisements. Headline journalists and marketing copy-writers know that sensational soundbites sell. Their headings need to pack more of a punch than those of their rivals. When Kylie Minogue was threatened by a stalker, *The Sun* summed up the story with the heading: '**I'LL KILL KYLIE**.' Notice the intricate pattern:

  I'll kill | Kylie
   I k /l | k /l

One summer, a poet from Wales was invited to Derry to address a forum on Celtic traditions. Eager to show that *cynghanedd* is a vibrant form, he was delighted to find in a newsagent on the way to the conference, the *Irish Mirror* carry a front-page story about a wild cat under the heading: '**Pu**ma **Paw**marks'!

The broad sheets such as *The Times* and *The Telegraph* have also been known to use this device in their publications. *The Times* once proudly praised the English cricket captain with the sentence: '**Huss**ein plays captains **inn**ings'. When the same captain decided some months later that the job was not for him, the seven-syllable line that was seen in many papers and heard in radio and television news headlines was '**Nass**er **Huss**ein has **res**igned.'

Another example of *cynghanedd* on the sports pages was seen when Eric Cantona, the French international who played for Manchester United, was convicted of kicking a Crystal Palace fan during a particularly heated game. The following day, one headline declared that Cantona could be expelled from the game '. . . **FOR KUNG FU KICKING** A **FAN**.' And what about *The Sun*'s unforgettable praise of France's 3-0 victory over Brazil in the 1998 World Cup: 'Defeat: **Zidane**'s **zidone** it'!

Perhaps it is less astonishing to find Huw Llywelyn Davies, Wales's best-known rugby commentator, and a deeply cultured man, using *cynghanedd* to bring the game alive. Once, during a test match between Australia and the Lions, one of the Lions had just kicked a high 'up-and-under' deep into the Australians' twenty-two. David Campese, the Austalian fullback watched the ball as it flew down towards him. He caught the ball under immense pressure and dispatched it fifty yards downfield into touch. Such a graceful piece of rugby skill needed an equally graceful line of description from the Welsh commentator, who duly delivered: '**Camp**ese, such com**po**sure'!

Then again, in advertising, *cynghanedd* is found time and again in slogans such as: '**Sp**ons**o**red by Marks and **Sp**enc**e**r', 'You'll be am**az**ed at a **Mazd**a', and the line aimed at children in the Granada service stations: '**D**e**nn**is the **Men**ace **Men**u' and its '**Gn**ash**e**r **Gn**osh up'!

It would be interesting to know whether all these examples of *cynghanedd* were accidental. Did Mac'n Ernies decide on the basis of *cerdd dafod* to introduce a line of '**Al**coho**lic** Co**la**'? Did Frank Hancock, when he established his brewery in Cardiff, realise that his name would be honoured forever in the line of *Cynghanedd Lusg*, 'Be fr**ank**, ask for H**anc**ocks?' And was that ageless caveman, Fred Flintsone, even before the time of Aneirin and Taliesin, the very first person ever to utter a line of *Cynghanedd Sain* in those immortal words, '**Y**abba **D**abba **D**oo!' We shall never know!

CHAPTER 7

Singing in Chains

People often ask poets where do their poems come from. The answers, usually after a long pause, vary. 'They grow from an idea in the imagination'; or 'they are inspired . . . sometimes by a feeling', '. . . sometimes by an observation', '. . . sometimes by an event', '. . . sometimes by an occasion' ('sometimes by a deadline or a commission!') 'Sometimes they start with a sound'.

Cynghanedd can be applied to each of these 'sometimes' scenarios, for as with all the other tools in the poet's kit, it is a means of pronouncing a thought in a way that lifts words from everyday expression. Poetry gives language a new dimension. But it is the last of the 'sometimes' listed above, the one that says 'sometimes they start with a sound', that is perhaps the most exciting of all in terms of *cynghanedd*. For the very process of searching for the sounds of *cynghanedd* can in itself lead the imagination to an idea. '*Chwilio am air a chael mwy*'. This line of *cynghanedd groes* reminds us of such a process – 'searching for a word, one finds more'.

One of the great pleasures I have had recently is visiting primary schools to teach *cynghanedd* to young Welsh speakers. Time and again I have been amazed by how the process of searching for words to form *cynghanedd* with other words opens the imagination's door. In one school I asked an eight-year-old pupil for a word, any word. He gave me '*oer*', the Welsh for 'cold'. I then asked his friend for a word that rhymed with '*oer*'; he promptly offered the word '*lloer*', 'moon'. With the two rhyming elements in place, we now needed a word that had the same pattern as '*lloer*', namely '*ll r*' in order to form *cynghanedd sain*, and in a split second the third pupil along suggested '*llaw*', 'hand'.

We put them together in a seven-syllable line and came up with '*mor oer yw'r lloer yn fy llaw*', 'the moon is so cold in my hand'. I praised the class. And then, to tease out an idea for a poem, I wore a very puzzled face and said 'But oh dear, it doesn't make sense. We can't hold the moon in our hand. What on earth could this be about?' With that, one of the children, who up to then hadn't uttered a word, put up an indignant hand and said 'But it does if we write a poem about a winter's night'.

And so we did.

The need to obey the strict rules of *cynghanedd* liberates the imagination. The chains both create the song and set it free. This is the tension of *cynghanedd*, the paradox that makes it such a force of creativity. It has a dynamic that both follows the train of thought and leads it.

When Ceri Wyn Jones, *Prifardd* and patient editor of this handbook, noticed the title of the painting for the book's cover *Mewn Cadwyni*, 'In Chains', his trained ear led him to comment quietly *'adenydd mewn cadwyni',* a perfect line of *cynghanedd draws* that translated means 'wings in chains'.

I believe the artist, Ozi Rhys Osmond, had something of this contradiction in mind when he painted the series of big heavy chests chained to the sea floor. He told me once that the symbolic chest contains 'the potential of Wales'. The chains in his painting however are nothing like the rules of *cynghanedd*. The chains that hold the chest only restrict and do not liberate. They are the forces that over the centuries have tried unsuccessfully to drown the Welsh voice.

All over the world noble languages and cultures of minorities are today singing in chains, as they struggle against a tide that seems determined to wash away all that is different and unique. Voices are being silenced, sometimes by violent winds, sometimes by seemingly gentle breezes.

The Welsh language is one of this threatened band. To date however, it has managed to keep its head above water. It has withstood countless threatening storms. And one of the buoys that has kept it afloat, has been its literature, its poetry and *cynghanedd*.

For those who wish to find out more about *cynghanedd*, a short bibliography is offered at the end of this book. You can also surf the web. There are approximately 3,000 website addresses that claim to throw some light on the craft, but beware! As is often the case on the internet, many of these are far from sound, and some offer concocted examples in English, that claim to be *cynghanedd* but are in fact nothing of the sort.

A short anthology of poetry in *cynghanedd* follows this chapter, offered with translations to guide the reader who doesn't yet speak

Welsh. Along with the poems and lines already quoted in the book, this anthology can be heard on the accompanying CD. Remember, it is the listening that is important, so try reading the texts aloud in their original form. Open your ears to their music . . . and above all, do start learning Welsh to appreciate their meaning!

CHAPTER 8

When Craft Becomes Art

I start this last chapter with Robert Frost, the American poet quoted in the first chapter. It is he who said 'Poetry is what is lost in translation. It is also what is lost in interpretation.' And he is probably right.

Translating poems is at best a difficult task. Translating poems written in *cynghanedd* is well nigh impossible. As I suggested earlier, it can be compared with attempting to translate a song, where not only the words but also the music must change, leaving virtually nothing in common with the original piece.

Despite this, while there is no attempt at interpretation in this chapter, I have included translations to guide the reader. They are the work of acknowledged experts who have overcome many of the hurdles in this difficult undertaking. The poems themselves are by three of the finest Welsh poets, each with a distinct voice.

The first poem is in fact three extracts from the *awdl 'Gwawr'* ('Dawn') by the *Prifardd* Emyr Lewis. He himself is the translator. This is followed by the series of *englynion* that opens the *awdl* 'Cilmeri' by the *Prifardd* Gerallt Lloyd Owen and translated by Professor Dafydd Johnston. The last poem is a shorter piece, a *cywydd* by Waldo Williams translated by Tony Conran entitled '*Daw'r Wennol yn ôl i'w Nyth*' ('The Swallow Will Find its Nest').

Waldo Williams, poet and pacifist, was born one hundred years ago. The *cywydd* quoted here ends with an affirmation of hope so typical of Waldo. He predicts the return of the swallow despite winter, the return of peace despite war. It is my privilege to close the book on this note.

Cywyddau from 'Gwawr'

Gwynt gwyllt fel magnet o'i go'
o le i le'n chwyrlïo,
yn poeri hen bapurau
hyd y stryd, a'r storiàu
fu ddoe mor ddwys a phwysig
yn y mwd yn chwarae mig
â sborion gwlyb disberod
dinas y baw, hyd nes bod
rhu diystyr didestun
dwsinau o eiriau'n un.

Wele'n awr y ddalen hon
oedd yn waedd o newyddion,
fu'n dyrnu brawl y deyrnas;
uwd brith yw'r penawdau bras.

Hen boer yw trên y bore,
ffag a llwch a diffyg lle,
ei lawn o benelinau
a deg yn eisteddle dau,
gwŷr blin mewn seti'n swta
heb air doeth na 'bore da',
yn rhannu gwg ar drên gwawr,
haid golledig y llwydwawr . . .

. . . 'Hwn yw fy llyfr, yn fy llaw
y treuliwyd ei ledr hylaw,
rhwygwyd lliain ei feingefn
wedi'r oes o ddweud y drefn,

Cywyddau from *'Gwawr'*

'Mad Magnet of a Wild Wind'

Mad magnet of a wild wind
here and there whirlying,
spittering old newspapers
along the street, the stories
(yesterday so grand and weighty)
are playing touch in the mud
with the detritus, stray and wet,
of dirt city, until the
meaningless, textless roaring
of countless words becomes one.

See now this page-leaf
which was a shout of news,
which pounded the kingdom's boast;
great headlines are grey stodge.

'Stale Spit is the Morning Train'

Stale spit is the morning train
fag and dust and lack of space,
brimming over with elbows
and ten in a seat made for two,
cross men, grumpy in their seats
no wise word, no good morning,
frown-sharing on daybreak's train,
the lost crowd of the grey dawn.

'This is My Book . . .'
(Old man's song)

'This is my book, in my hand
its handy leather has worn,
its spinecloth has ripped after
an age of laying down law,

ei feinwe'n dadelfennu
yn dwll dan y cloriau du,
a throi'n niwl lythrennau aur
eglured gynt ar gloriau'r
hen erfyn cydymffurfiaeth
ddefnyddiwn i gadw'n gaeth
gymaint o saint ar y Sul
yng nghrafangau'r Efengyl.

'Hon yw coler cywilydd,
iwniffòrm fy nhipyn ffydd,
hon yw y siwt wisgais i'n
addurn ym mhob cwrdd gweddi,
ei 'dafedd sy'n nadreddu,
aeth yn dwll ei brethyn du.

'Cerddaf lle nad oes cyrddau
yn dawel drwy'r capel cau
ynysig o fydysawd,
drwy'r ddinas, heb ras na brawd;
ym mynwent ei phalmentydd
llwyd y diffoddwyd fy ffydd.
Nid yw edau y Duwdod
yn bwyth drwy frethyn ein bod.'

O'i gwmpas y mae sasiwn
hynod y cathod a'r cŵn.

Yn ei ben mae bachgen bach
yn heulwen oes siriolach
yn cydio dwylo ei dad,
dwylo cawr, dwylo cariad;
dau rith hyd rith o draethell
yn haul poeth gorffennol pell . . .

From *Chwarae Mig*, Emyr Lewis, Cyhoeddiadau Barddas

its tissue decomposing
to a hole under dark covers,
turning to fog the golden
letters once so clear on the
old tool of conformity
I wielded to keep captive
so many saints of a Sunday
in the gospel's clutches.

This is the collar of shame,
uniform of my bit-faith,
this is the suit which I wore,
adornment in each prayer meeting,
its threads snaking apart,
its black fabric has become a hole.

I walk where there are no meetings,
silent through the universe's
remote, deserted chapel,
through the graceless, brotherless city,
in whose graveyard-grey pavements
my faith was snuffed out.
The Godhead's thread does not run
one stitch through our living weave."

About him is the peculiar
synod of cats and dogs.

In his head is a small boy
in sunsmile of more cheerful times
holding his father's hands,
hands of a giant, hands of love,
two ghosts along the ghost of a beach
in the hot sun of a distant past.

Translated by Emyr Lewis
From *Modern Poetry in Translation*, King's College, London

From 'Cilmeri'

Yn fraw agos ar frigyn
Gwelaf leuad llygadwyn
Mor oer â'r marw ei hun

A diddiffodd ddioddef
Y byw yn ei wyneb ef
Yn felynllwyd fel hunllef.

Wyneb y diwedd unig,
Druan rhwth, uwch dyrnau'r wig
Yn geudod dirmygedig.

Hyd eithaf y ffurfafen
Y teimlaf ei anaf hen
A'i wae ym mhob gwythïen.

Er bod bysedd y beddau
Yn deilwriaid doluriau,
Cnawd yn y co' nid yw'n cau.

Â chof sy'n hwy na chofio fe welaf
Eilwaith ddydd ei lorio
Ac ail-fyw ei glwyfau o
Â galar hŷn nag wylo.

Hwn yw'r cof am wylofain awyr wag
A'r tir oll yn gelain;
Rhagfyr drwy'r goedwig frigfain
A'i drwst megis ffaglau drain.

Wybren y bore'n aberoedd o waed
Yn hollt y mynyddoedd;
Gwridog fel dagr ydoedd
Y wawr, a gwawr euog oedd.

Yntau yn llaes ei fantell, ŵr unig
Ar riniog ei babell,
A roddodd goel ar ddydd gwell,
A hen gam yn ei gymell.

From 'Cilmeri'

Terrifyingly close over the treetops
I see a white-eyed moon
as cold as a dead man

with the unending suffering
of the living in his face,
yellowish-grey like a nightmare.

The face of the lone death,
the hollow stare of a despised wretch
above the wood's fists.

To the very limits of the sky
I feel his old injury
and his agony in every vein.

Although the grave's fingers
are skilled tailors of wounds,
in the memory the flesh still gapes.

With a memory longer than mere remembering
I see again the day he was cut down
and I relive his wounds
with a grief older than tears.

This is the memory of an empty sky lamenting
and all the land a corpse;
December through the emaciated trees
crackling like blazing thorns.

The morning sky awash with blood
from the gash in the mountains;
the dawn was flushed like a dagger,
and it was a guilty dawn.

He stood wrapped in his cloak,
a lonely figure at the door of his tent,
one who put his faith in a better dawn,
driven by an old wrong.

Hon oedd gwawr fawr ei fwriad a hawliai
Orwelion ei dreftad;
I'w golau hi deffrôi gwlad,
Hi oedd diwedd dyhead . . .

From *Cilmeri a Cherddi Eraill,* Gerallt Lloyd Owen, Gwasg Gwynedd

This was the great dawn of his design
which would reclaim the horizons of his inheritance;
by its light a land would awaken,
it would fulfil all yearning . . .

Translated by Dafydd Johnston
From *Modern Poetry in Translation*, King's College, London

Daw'r Wennol yn ôl i'w Nyth

Daw'r wennol yn ôl i'w nyth,
O'i haelwyd â'r wehelyth.
Derfydd calendr yr hendref
A'r teulu a dry o dref,
Pobl yn gado bro eu bryd,
Tyf hi'n wyllt a hwy'n alltud.
Bydd truan hyd lan Lini
Ei hen odidowgrwydd hi.

Hwylia o'i nawn haul y nef,
Da godro nis dwg adref.
Gweddw buarth heb ei gwartheg,
Wylofain dôl a fu'n deg.
Ni ddaw gorymdaith dawel
Y buchod sobr a'u gwobr gêl;
Ni ddaw dafad i adwy
Ym Mhen yr Hollt na mollt mwy.

Darfu hwyl rhyw dyrfa wen
O dorchiad y dywarchen,
Haid ewynlliw adeinllaes,
Gŵyr o'r môr gareio'r maes.
Mwy nid ardd neb o'r mebyd
Na rhannu grawn i'r hen grud.
I'w hathrofa daeth rhyfel
I rwygo maes Crug y Mêl.

Mae parabl y stabl a'i stŵr,
Tynnu'r gwair, gair y gyrrwr?
Peidio'r pystylad cadarn,
Peidio'r cur o'r pedwar carn;
Tewi'r iaith ar y trothwy
A miri'r plant, marw yw'r plwy.
Gaeaf ni bydd tragyfyth.
Daw'r wennol yn ôl i'w nyth.

From *Dail Pren,* Waldo Williams, Gomer

The Swallow will find her Nest

The swallow will find her nest,
But kinship leaves the fireside.
Calendar of the homestead
Finished, and the family fled,
People letting the land go wild,
From their heart's country exiled.
A poor thing splendour will be
Along the banks of Lini.

Sun sails from noon, but homeward
Plods no more the milking herd.
The yard's reft of cattle, and woe
To the once-lovely meadow.
The sober cows' procession
With their offering, will not come;
Nor in Pen-yr-Hollt you'll see
The sheep come to the valley.

No more a white crowd's sportive
At the turning of the turf –
Foam-white swarm, trail-winged, they know
Far at sea, a field's in furrow.
No one young ploughs now at all,
Sows seed to the old cradle.
To that school of theirs, war's come –
Crug y Mêl field ripped open.

Where's the stable talk, muttered
Lugging hay, the driver's word?
Ended the strong stamp of feet,
Ended the fourfold hoofbeat.
The language dumb at doorway,
Parish dead, no children play.
But winter won't be endless.
The swallow will find its nest.

From *The Peacemakers*, Waldo Williams, Gomer
Translated by Tony Conran

Solutions

Exercise 1 (page 29)

SIR, SEREN, SIRIOL, SIWR, SAWR, SAER
DWYLO, DWL, DOLI, ADEILAD
PÊL, POLYN, PWYLAIDD, PYLU

Exercise 2 (page 35)

Un awr harddach na'r hwyrddydd
A mi'n fawr y mae'n fyrrach
Roedd eira ar y dderwen
A breuddwyd heb arwyddion

Exercise 3 (page 39)

Eiliadau yw pob blodyn
Awyr goch yn friwiau i gyd*
Os ydwyf yn drwsiadus
Yma nawr yng nghwmni neb

*cf. Chapter 4 page 52 – *ceseilio*

Exercise 4 (page 43)

Ac fe ddaeth yn gaeth a gwan
Y gwarth a'r trais deimlaist di
Ar draws gwlad mewn dillad du
Rwy'n galw ei henw hi

Exercise 5 (page 46)

Heb amserlen na threnau
Lladd hyder yng Nghilmeri
Mor dawel oedd Llywelyn
Ond cyn bedd dyma 'ngweddi

Further Reading

Odl a Chynghanedd, Dewi Emrys, London (1938)

Cerdd Dafod, John Morris Jones, Oxford (1925)

Anghenion y Gynghanedd, Alan Lloyd Roberts (Alan Llwyd), Cardiff (1973)

Clywed Cynghanedd, Myrddin ap Dafydd, Llanrwst (1994)

Y Cynganeddion Cymreig, David Thomas, Wrexham (1923)

Yr Ysgol Farddol, Dafydd Morgannwg, Carmarthen

Celtic Word Craft, Idwal Lloyd, Redruth (1985)

A pocket guide to the Literature of Wales, Dafydd Johnston, Cardiff (1994)

A pocket guide to the Welsh Language, Janet Davies, Cardiff (1999)

A pocket guide to the History of Wales, J. Graham Jones, Cardiff (1998)

The Bloodaxe Book of Modern Welsh Poetry, edited by Menna Elfyn and John Rowlands, Northumberland (2003)

Llawlyfr y Cynganeddion, J. J. Evans, Cardiff (1951)

The Eisteddfod, Hywel Teifi Edwards, Cardiff (1990) (Writers of Wales, series editors Meic Stephens and R. Brinley Jones)

Modern Poetry in Translation, no 7 Welsh Spring 1995, guest editor Dafydd Johnston, general editor Daniel Weissbort, London (1995)

Poetry Wales, Summer 1978, Volume 14 no 1, Swansea (1978), editor J. P. Ward